Contents

Author's foreword 2

UK Edition

Copyright © 2006, 2016 text AG&G Books

Copyright © 2006, 2016 illustrations and photographs IMM Lifestyle Books

Copyright © 2006, 2016 IMM Lifestyle Books

Designed and created for IMM Lifestyle Books by AG&G Books. Copyright © 2004 "Specialist" AG&G Books

Design: Glyn Bridgewater; Illustrations: Dawn Brend, Gill Bridgewater, Coral Mula, and Ann Winterbotham; Editor: Alison Copland; Photographs: see page 80

Current Printing (last digit)

10 9 8 7 6 5 4 3 2 1

Printed in Singapore

Home Gardener's Garden Design & Planning: Designing, planning, building, planting, improving and maintaining gardens is published by Creative Homeowner under license with IMM Lifestyle Books.

ISBN: 978-1-58011-772-2

Creative Homeowner®, *www.creativehomeowner.com*, is distributed exclusively in the United Kingdom by Grantham Book Service, Trent Road, Grantham, Lincolnshire, NG31 7XQ.

Author's Foreword

The moment you take people out into the garden, they immediately become more relaxed and expansive. Their smiles get bigger, they talk more loudly, their hand movements are broader, and they generally stride around looking happier. Whoever said that the great outdoors is our natural habitat certainly knew what they were talking about. Gardens are uniquely wonderful.

What could be better after a hot, sticky day at work, or a long drive home, than to relax in the garden? Gardens are all things to all people – a place for reading, a place for growing tasty vegetables, a place for playing out private fantasies such as building a log cabin, digging holes, building ponds or breeding chickens, a place for whatever takes your fancy. Patios, ponds, sheds, chalets, barbecues, vegetable plots and lawns … there are so many exciting options.

Your garden might not be much bigger than a small room, but this does not mean that you cannot turn it into the best room in the house – a room with a ceiling that stretches right up to the sky. This book will gently guide you through all the stages, from planning and making drawings through to selecting tools, digging, building walls, planting, stocking and much more besides. No more dreaming … now is the time for turning fantasies into realities.

Measurements

Both metric and imperial measurements are given in this book – for example, 1.8 m (6 ft).

SEASONS

Because of global and even regional variations in climate and temperatures, throughout this book planting advice is given in terms of the four main seasons, with each subdivided into 'early', 'mid-' and 'late' – for example, early spring, mid-spring and late spring. These 12 divisions of the year can be applied to the approximate calendar months in your local area, if you find this helps.

About the Authors

Alan and Gill Bridgewater have gained an international reputation as producers of highly successful gardening and DIY books on a range of subjects, including garden design, ponds and patios, stone and brickwork, decks and decking, and household woodworking. They have also contributed to several international magazines. They live in Rye, East Sussex.

Enjoying your garden

Although you might start out with preconceived notions – the garden has to be formal, or you want to grow vegetables, for example – the finished garden will of necessity be a coming-together of what you dream of having and what you actually have on the ground – the location, the size of the plot, the character of your home, and so on. The best way of getting started is to list your needs, think hard about the possibilities, and take things from there.

How do I get the best out of my garden?

YOUR NEEDS

List your needs in order of priority. Your needs might be unspoken, but you probably know absolutely for sure what you *don't* want. If this is the case, then list what you don't want, and then, by a process of elimination, gradually work through to what you would like to have.

THE POSSIBILITIES

Look at the size and location of your plot, and the size of your bank balance, and consider the possibilities accordingly. You might want a huge lake, but if you only have a modest-sized garden, with a modest-sized bank balance to match, it is probably better to modify your 'needs' and opt for a good-sized pond.

IMPROVING AND EVOLVING

Gardens generally improve and evolve simply with the passing of time. Plants get bigger, new plants can be grown, lawns can be changed into flower beds, and so on.

Even the smallest patch can be turned into a gentle, soothing haven.

GARDENING STYLES

Although there are only two basic styles of garden, informal and formal, there are many variations on these styles. For example, you could have an informal cottage-orchard type garden, or an informal wild garden. Much the same goes for a formal garden. You could have a classic garden with all the features relating to a symmetrical ground plan, or you could have a Japanese garden that is formal in its layout.

Informal

↖ *Wildlife areas introduce a new dimension to gardening, and are perfect for a small, quiet, out-of-the-way position.*

↗ *A natural patio complete with apple trees and meadow grass.*

Formal

→ *A small formal garden which has been designed so that the plants can easily be changed to follow the seasons.*

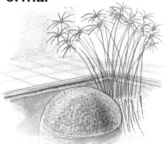

↗ *A single stone ball can be an eye-catching feature.*

Themed

↗ *Areas of gravel create the perfect base for a Japanese garden.*

Assessing your garden

Where do I start?

A successful garden is nearly always a marriage of what you actually have and what you would like to have. The first step is to spend time in the garden. Look at the space, the levels, the walls and so on, and then decide what you want from your garden. Do you like gardening, or do you simply want to enjoy being outdoors? Consider your finances and your physical capabilities. Generally think through the possibilities and then slowly begin to make plans.

SIZE

Garden size is relative. If you are not very keen on gardening and just want a space to relax and read a book, 0.2 of a hectare (half an acre) is a huge area, but if you want to grow all your own vegetables then the same area is perhaps a bit poky. Big, small, long or wide, treat the space like a room in your house and make the most of all the existing features.

SHAPE

Making the most of an unusually shaped space – thin, wide, triangular, L-shaped, or whatever – can result in a uniquely exciting garden. A difficult corner plot can be a problem, but then again such a shape offers you the chance to create a really unusual garden, one that stands out from its neighbours.

EXTREMELY SLOPING SITES

Extremely sloping sites can be great fun. You have three options. In ascending order of sweat and expense, you can make something of it as is, you can build raised decking to create level patio areas, and, most difficult of all, you can create one or more terraces. If you want terraces but need to keep costs down, and don't mind hard work, the best option is to cut and move the existing soil.

ORIENTATION

Stand in the garden at various times of the day, and look at the house and the trees and the position of the sun. As you cannot move the house within the site, you have no choice other than to design the garden so that it makes the most of what is on offer in the way of sun, shade and privacy. Decide, for example, if you want the patio in full sun, or the vegetable plot in full sun and yet out of sight of the house.

Design the garden so that it makes the most of the sun.

EXPOSED SITES

Ordinary garden plants hate wind. The key to creating a garden on an exposed site is to build as many windbreaks as possible – walls, fences, sheds and the like – and then to grow tough plants on the lea or sheltered side of the breaks. Once the plants are established, the enclosed space will be that much warmer and draught-free – a good environment for a whole range of medium to fully hardy plants.

SOIL TYPES

To a great extent, you have no choice but to work with your soil – its particular type and conditions. The soil type will influence what you can grow. Don't worry too much about its pH (whether it is acid or alkaline); just take note of whether it is sandy, wet, dry, clay or rocky, and then look around at your locality and choose plants that will thrive in that type of soil.

LARGE PERMANENT FEATURES

In most instances, you have to work around large permanent features such as a huge tree, the back of a neighbour's shed, a tall wall that overlooks the garden or a streetlight. If you don't like the back of the neighbour's shed, then why not block it out with a shed of your own, a trellis covered with a vigorous climbing plant, or a tall, attractive fence? Try to use the back of the shed to your advantage.

YOU AND YOUR GARDEN

The wonderful thing about gardens is that they give you the chance to create your own private haven. Of course, you do have to consider the needs of friends and neighbours, but first and foremost you must start by identifying your own needs – all the things that you do and don't want.

Balcony gardens

The best way of coping with a cramped balcony garden is to use a variety of containers; these may be fixed to the balustrade, used as windowboxes, hanging from the walls, arranged in tiers or in groups on the floor, placed in groups just inside the door to the house, and so on. Use container plants to blur the boundaries between the inside and outside space.

Roof gardens

Much depends upon the size of your roof garden, but as a generalization it is always a good decision to spend on a quality floor such as tiles or decking, really good furniture, and as many pots and containers as you can get into the space.

IDEAS SUITED TO THE TYPES OF GARDEN

Your garden might well be, in some way or other, uniquely tricky, but the good news is that there will be all sorts of exciting ideas and options that you can use to best advantage.

Small shady garden with moist soil Try a woodland theme with a small sitting area or 'glade' positioned to catch available patches of sunshine. Go for woodland plants that positively enjoy damp shady conditions, like ferns, ivies, some grasses and bamboos, hostas, *Polygonatum*, primulas and hydrangeas.

Small shady garden with dry soil A good idea is a woodland glade theme with shrubs and trees like fuchsias, *Parthenocissus* (Virginia creeper) and *Acers* (Japanese Maples) around the borders. Have a large patch of lawn for the 'glade'. Extend the woodland glade theme by spreading a mulch of woodchip around the shrubs and trees.

Small sunny garden with dry soil Position a chalet or bower so that it catches most of the sunshine, and then have a small pool with appropriate planting. You could have *Eichhornia* (Water Hyacinth), *Aponogeton distachyos* (Water Hawthorn) and a whole range of lilies.

Sloping garden with stony soil Take advantage of the stony conditions by making the garden into one large alpine rock garden. Bring in large feature rocks and stone troughs, and grow alpine plants like Thyme, *Sedum* (Stonecrop), *Iberis* (Candytuft) and *Phlox subulata* (Moss Phlox).

Large garden with wet clay soil Turn the whole garden into one big water garden with a large natural pond at the centre and areas of bog garden to catch the runoff from the pond. Have all the usual plants in the pond, with the marginals around the pond blurring into bog plants like irises, primulas, ferns and *Hemerocallis* (Daylilies).

Garden with back-to-back houses Position a chalet at the bottom of the garden, with trellis to each side, and then plant climbers to grow over it. You could concentrate on *Clematis* – search out the various spring, summer, autumn and winter varieties – so that you have foliage, buds and flowers all year.

Garden sloping down from the house Create a flat terrace area close to the house with steps running from the terrace down to the lawn and flowerbeds. You could have a cottage-garden feature in the lower garden with wildflowers like *Viola odorata* (Sweet Violet), *Lythrum salicaria* (Purple Loosestrife) and *Lychnis flos-cuculi* (Ragged Robin).

Garden sloping up from the house Dig out the ground close to the house and build a patio. You could have steps leading up the slope with ponds and waterfalls at various levels. The idea is that you can sit on the patio and view the water and plants as they cascade down the slope.

Small garden ringed by high walls Fix wires and trellises on all the walls and then plant a whole range of climbing plants. You could have *Parthenocissus* (Virginia Creeper) and *Pileostegia viburnoides* on the shady walls, and plants like *Wisteria* and *Lonicera* (Honeysuckle) where there is sun.

Small walled courtyard garden Build a pergola that more or less fills the space. Cover the top of the pergola with clear plastic sheet so that the courtyard is roofed over. Put a small wall feature on one wall, and plant grapevines on the underside of the pergola so you can sit out in all weathers.

Wish list

Every good idea starts with a wish list. The very act of sitting and dreaming about what is possible is a good part of the pleasure of gardening. I wish I could have …

Barbecue: a brick-built barbecue is a good option. All you need is a patio area, the barbecue itself and seating all around.

Beds and borders: beds and borders are like an ever-changing film screen – places that you can stuff full of colour.

Bird bath and bird table: bird baths and tables are a must. What better way to enjoy the garden in winter than to put food out and to watch the birds feeding and bathing?

Chalet: lots of people dream about having a chalet. Just think about it – a place for the kids, or a place for sleeping when the weather is hot and sticky.

Chickens: going to the chicken house and listening to that very special sound that hens make when they are about to lay … it's a thought!

Fruit trees: apples and plums are good, but when they are fresh from the tree they are very special – a gift from nature.

Greenhouse: if you want to be able to get out into the garden from very early spring until early winter, you are going to need a greenhouse.

Herb garden: a sunny patio is good, but a patio planted with herbs such as thyme, sage, marjoram and so on is better.

Kids' garden: children need a place to play. A climbing frame is fine, but a place to dig and make a camp, and make a mess, is so much better.

Lawn: an area of lawn is essential. The mowing may be a bit of a chore, but the scent given off by the freshly cut grass, and the pleasure of sitting on the lawn, are experiences that should not be missed.

Log cabin: if ever there was a dream feature, this is it. It can be just about anything you care to make it – a workshop, a weekend cabin, a place for the kids, or a potting shed.

Patio: what could be more pleasurable on a warm sunny day than to sit on a patio with friends and family? A good patio is a choice item.

Pergola: a well-placed pergola is another great option – good for providing shade over the patio, for growing grapes and for blotting out eyesores.

Pond: water has irresistible magical qualities that give us pleasure – the sight and sound of moving water is fascinating.

Raised beds: raised beds not only make for easy gardening – with less strain on the back – but they are also good for keeping small toddlers and pets away from the plants.

Summerhouse: a summerhouse is a delightful setting for having afternoon tea, reading a good book or just indulging in some quiet contemplation.

Vegetable plot: this is the age of the vegetable plot. If you enjoy fresh food and/or want to go organic, then a vegetable garden is for you.

Wildlife: birds, bugs, frogs, toads, newts and small mammals … a wildlife garden is one of life's great pleasures.

Gathering inspiration

Where do I start?

In much the same way as poets and artists draw inspiration from their interests and passions – romantic love, the glories of nature, the wonders of technology, travel – so the garden designer needs to draw inspiration from his or her experiences and passions. Whatever your interests may be – trees, roses, water, travel, eating in the garden, watching your children at play – your best starting point is to draw inspiration from the things that give you pleasure.

LOOKING AND COLLECTING

Note the large, permanent objects and items that you have to live with, such as the house, boundary walls and large trees, and then look around you at the things you have collected. For example, you might have a collection of nautical bits like anchors, glass floats and chains, old street lamps, old farm items, special plants or perhaps even your holiday photographs to inspire you.

A collection of bamboos could well be inspirational.

Favourite plants can also provide great inspiration.

Try found objects such as Victorian street lamps.

Postcards of beautiful gardens will give you something to aim for.

Books, magazines and television programmes

Once you have come up with the bare bones of a scheme, follow through your research by looking through books and magazines, and by watching television. It is a good idea to make a collection of the ideas that you would like to include in your design – colours, plants, materials, structures, furniture, in fact anything and everything that strikes your fancy.

Keep a scrapbook. Save photographs from magazines and catalogues that show things like grand houses, holidays, flowers or sculpture.

Garden centres and nurseries

Garden centres and nurseries are great places for searching out ideas. Arm yourself with a digital camera, paper and pencil, and take note of everything that looks interesting. Gather a body of data to flesh out and back up your ideas – names of plants, colours, growing habits and so on. If you have in mind to go for a theme, say a Japanese garden, search out plants, materials and products that you know to be variously useful, traditional or characteristic.

Wander around the garden centre or nursery keeping an eye open for anything that might spark an idea, such as unusual containers.

As you walk slowly around the various displays, take photographs of plants, products and features that you think might fit well into your scheme.

Visiting gardens

If you have a friend who has created a beautiful garden, when you next visit ask them to tell you about how they got started and how the design has evolved.

It is also a good idea to visit world-renowned gardens that are open to the public. In the UK, for example, there are the Royal Horticultural Society (RHS) grounds at Wisley and Hyde Hall, and various grand house gardens may be found throughout the world. The RHS gardens are particularly interesting in that they have gardens that have been designed by celebrated designers and experts.

A fine example of a traditional English pergola, with solid square-section brick columns topped off with oak beams.

A well-planted border can be a joy to the eye – so stunning that you might want to copy it in every detail.

Sometimes a particular arrangement of plants and structures, such as this piece of statuary placed beneath a rose arch, is inspiration enough.

Plants you like

List your favourite plants, with common names and botanical names, and brief details about their growing habits. Try to get magazine images as a reference. Ask friends, family and neighbours to tell you as much as they can about them.

Unsuitable plants

Look at your list in the light of your designs, and cross out ones that are obviously unsuitable. You might like the colour and the scent, but if it is going to grow too big for your space, or it is too prickly for say a child's play area, then it is no good. Size and habit are particularly important if you are designing a small, enclosed garden.

OTHER SOURCES OF INSPIRATION

Famous paintings Paintings are inspirational. For example, how about a garden design based on one of Monet's lily-pond paintings?

Memories Rolling around in your grandfather's apple orchard, flirting under a particular type of tree … these types of memories can be particularly inspirational.

Fantasies If, for example, you have fantasies about living in a hut on a tropical island, you could build the fantasy into your designs.

Country walks A bend in a river with a quaint wooden bridge and willows … country walks are another rich source of ideas.

Cultural influences If you have experienced the pleasures of sitting in a Mediterranean garden, or under a loggia in India, why not create one of your own?

PUTTING THE ELEMENTS TOGETHER

Something for everyone in the family It is important to include the whole family in the design process – adults, children and even pets. Make sure everyone is happy with the end design.
Deciding what to drop If you have worries, such as the kids falling into the pond or plant allergies, then simply leave these elements out of the design.
Eclectic or sweet harmony? Most gardens veer towards harmony but, if you know what you like and you want a glorious unrelated mishmash of styles and forms, the choice is yours.
Scaling down Sometimes you do have to compromise. If an element is dangerously large, or there just is not enough room for all those oak trees, you have no choice but to scale down.
Cost and time When it comes down to it, most designs hinge on money and time. You could spread the creation time over several years, get friends to help with the work and beg and borrow plants, but you might also need to cut basic material costs – stone, wood, cement and the like.

Design techniques

This is the exciting bit. You have visited grand houses and show gardens, taken many photographs, developed a passion for just about everything, and generally looked, collected and clipped until your mind is racing with ideas. When it comes to good design, it helps if you follow the rule that says 'form follows function'. This means that your final design should be a balanced blend of both your functional needs and your ideas and passions.

A long, formal pond or canal links the patio with the rest of the garden. The natural earth-coloured bricks and symmetrical layout give this design a traditional or classic feel. The planting is less formal.

A decking patio with seaside overtones – the matching raised beds are topped with turquoise crushed stone to draw the eye. This is an entirely modern design that focuses on colour, texture and function.

GOOD DESIGN, POOR DESIGN, TASTE AND STYLE

In the context of design, a good starting point is to say that things and structures have to work – gates must open, seating needs to be comfortable, steps must be safe, and so on. If you are worried about what constitutes good taste or good style, then the best advice is to relate to tried and trusted classical forms. If you go for untried, cutting-edge forms and imagery, then you may risk, certainly in the short term, your design being described as being in poor taste or poor style – sometimes possibly for no other reason than that it has not passed the test of time.

DRAWING INSPIRATION FROM AN EXISTING DESIGN

There is a fine line between drawing inspiration from an existing design and copying a design. If you visit a garden and are so excited by it that you go away and create a garden that pays homage to it, you are drawing inspiration from it. If, however, you replicate it stone by stone and flower by flower, you are merely copying it.

FRESH, ORIGINAL IDEAS

Using fresh, original ideas is always good. Try to be original with the small things – the little details – and big original ideas should follow. There is no credit in being original just for the sake of it, however. Of course, it is always good to aim for originality, but do not worry too much if you fail.

GARDENS EVOLVE

The wonderful thing about gardens is the way they evolve. You start by putting in structures – paths, walls, and hard areas – and gradually as plants grow in size and number, and as your behaviour changes, so you will find that you will, almost by necessity, modify the shape of the structures to fit.

Harmony and contrast

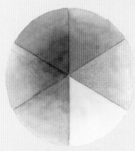

You can use a colour wheel like this to help you make informal decisions.

Taken literally, the term 'harmony' describes forms, colours and textures that are similar one to another, to the extent that they look happy together. Red brick, stone and wood might be described as being in harmony. The term 'contrast' describes forms, textures and colours that are dissimilar or opposite. The strange thing is that contrasts – say dark against light, or rough against smooth – can be a joy to the eye. For example, polished marble can look all the more exciting when it is set against a contrasting material like rough-hewn oak.

LANDSCAPING TIPS

Work with what you have: do your best to keep and use what you have – mature trees, dips and hollows in the ground, natural features like rocks and pools.

Soil stability: be wary about making big changes with wet or waterlogged soil, or soil on a sloping site. Take advice if you have doubts.

The house must look comfortable: aim for a landscape that holds and nestles the house, so that the house looks 'happy' in its setting.

Get the best viewpoint: shape the garden so that it looks its best when seen from the house. If you get it right, the house will also look its best from various vantage points around the garden.

Draw inspiration from nature: the easiest way forward is to draw inspiration from a slice of nature – a forest glade, a valley, the side of a hill.

Materials in harmony: all new materials look their best when they are drawn from the locality – local bricks, local stone, local wood.

Scale in harmony: aim for structures that complement the house in size, rather than structures that overwhelm the house.

PLANTING TIPS

If you liken planting to painting colours on a canvas, you can take the analogy one step further by saying that you must hold back with the planting until the canvas – the structure of the garden – has been well prepared.

Climatic conditions: the plants must be suitable for your climate – it is no good going for delicate plants if your site is windy and subject to frosts.

Soil conditions: the plants must suit the soil – you must not choose chalk-loving plants if your soil is predominantly clay.

Sun and shade conditions: look at the way the sun moves around the garden, note the areas that are sunny and shady, and position the plants accordingly.

Scale: take note of the potential size of plants – the width and height when fully grown. Be especially wary of some of the fast-growing conifers.

Year-round colour: aim for a broad selection of plants, so that you have year-round foliage, bud, stem and flower colour.

Container-grown plants: these can be purchased and planted all year round.

MAKING NOTES AND SKETCHES

It is a good idea to go out into your garden, with a stack of coloured pens and a pad of gridded paper, and to make sketches. Take measurements of the garden, decide on the scale – say one grid square equals 60 cm (2 ft) – and then draw the garden in plan and perspective view, with close-up details showing special areas of interest (see right). Draw what you already have, and then draw in any desired changes. Try to visualize how the changes will affect how you use the space. Place markers around the garden so that you can more easily visualize changes.

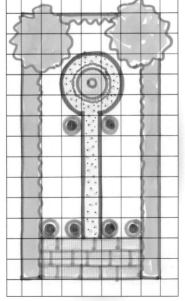

A perspective view of the garden is more difficult to draw than a plan view, but is nevertheless the best way to visualize your design.

Use a rope, hosepipe or chain together with some pegs to help you plot out an irregular shape.

A plan view of the garden (viewed from above) can be drawn to scale over gridded paper. Colouring in areas can be helpful.

Important features can be drawn separately and in more detail.

Getting it down on paper

How do I make a working drawing?

If you want the project to run smoothly, you need to plan everything out and make drawings. The procedure is as follows: first, make a rough sketch on a scrap of paper, showing the existing garden with measurements. Next, transfer these details onto graph paper to make a 'site plan' (drawn to scale). Then, set a sheet of gridded paper over the site plan and make a 'master plan' of the new garden, tracing the boundaries and existing items as required.

MAKING THE SITE PLAN

About graph paper You will need a pad of graph layout paper – meaning thin paper that has been printed with a grid – the biggest size of pad that you can obtain. Look at the size of your garden; say it is 30 m (100 ft) long and 25 m (80 ft) wide, and decide on the scale of your gridded paper. Count the squares on the long side of the paper and divide them by the length of the garden. Work to the nearest whole square. So, for example, if the paper is 100 squares long, then you could say that one square on the paper equals 30 cm (1 ft) in the garden.

Measuring your garden Use a long tape measure to measure your garden. Start by measuring the length. Plot this measurement on the long side of the paper. Repeat the procedure with the width of the garden and plot it on the short side of the paper.

Right angles – 90° angles Check for right angles by measuring the diagonals. For example, if your garden is in any way square or rectilinear, then the crossed diagonal measurements should more or less be equal.

Awkward shapes You can plot an awkward shape by drawing a straight line from two fixed points – say between two trees. Step off at regular intervals along the straight line and measure how far the curves of the awkward shape are out from the stepped-off point.

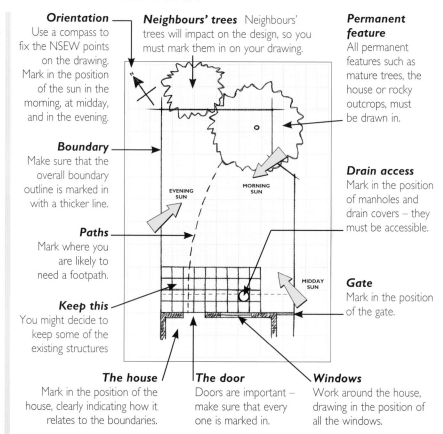

Orientation Use a compass to fix the NSEW points on the drawing. Mark in the position of the sun in the morning, at midday, and in the evening.

Neighbours' trees Neighbours' trees will impact on the design, so you must mark them in on your drawing.

Permanent feature All permanent features such as mature trees, the house or rocky outcrops, must be drawn in.

Boundary Make sure that the overall boundary outline is marked in with a thicker line.

Drain access Mark in the position of manholes and drain covers – they must be accessible.

Paths Mark where you are likely to need a footpath.

Keep this You might decide to keep some of the existing structures

Gate Mark in the position of the gate.

EVENING SUN

MORNING SUN

MIDDAY SUN

The house Mark in the position of the house, clearly indicating how it relates to the boundaries.

The door Doors are important – make sure that every one is marked in.

Windows Work around the house, drawing in the position of all the windows.

Items that you need to mark in on the site plan

- NSEW
- Midday sun
- Outline of boundary
- Items that you want to keep or modify
- House
- Mature trees
- Neighbours' trees
- Underground pipes and cables
- Doors on house
- Windows on house
- Drain access points
- Main gate

Paths and drives

If the site plan is a record of items and structures that you have no choice but to leave unchanged, you have the option here of whether or not to mark in the position of the paths and drives. You could say that, since the position of the front door and the front gate are fixed, it follows that the paths will also stay the same. This does not necessarily follow, however. That said, it is usually a good idea to draw them in.

Slopes in cross-section

The easiest way of recording a slope is to draw a cross-section view. Draw the length of the slope on a piece of graph paper and label the line 'top'. You need a spirit (carpenter's) level taped to a 2 m (7 ft) long batten. Working from the top of the slope, hold one end of the batten on the ground so that the level is true, and measure the vertical distance from the overhanging end of the batten down to the ground. Mark this in on the drawing. Continue down the slope until you have a record.

MAKING THE MASTER PLAN

Tracing the site plan Put a sheet of graph paper over the site plan and use the underlying plan to work out what you want in your new garden. You might well have to go through this procedure a dozen or so times before you have a drawing that suits all your needs.

Pencilling in your design Once you have achieved a good preliminary plan, set it under another sheet of graph paper and trace it off with a pencil. This new drawing is your 'master plan'. You should now have two finished drawings – the site plan that records the bare bones of the garden, and the master plan that sets out the design of the new garden. You can photocopy the master plan so you have lots of copies.

Separate details Some items are so complex in themselves that they will need working drawings. So, for example, with a water feature, you will need a plan view, a front view and a cross-section showing how it is constructed.

Colouring in Some people make coloured drawings to show how the garden might look at various times of the year. To make a coloured drawing, set a sheet of plain paper over the master plan – hold it against a window and make a tracing. Tint this drawing with coloured pencils or watercolours.

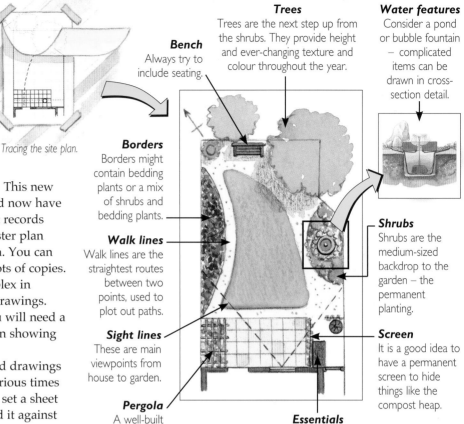

Tracing the site plan.

Bench Always try to include seating.

Trees Trees are the next step up from the shrubs. They provide height and ever-changing texture and colour throughout the year.

Water features Consider a pond or bubble fountain – complicated items can be drawn in cross-section detail.

Borders Borders might contain bedding plants or a mix of shrubs and bedding plants.

Walk lines Walk lines are the straightest routes between two points, used to plot out paths.

Sight lines These are main viewpoints from house to garden.

Pergola A well-built pergola provides shade.

Shrubs Shrubs are the medium-sized backdrop to the garden – the permanent planting.

Screen It is a good idea to have a permanent screen to hide things like the compost heap.

Essentials All gardens need little corners for hiding away items such as old tools, sticks and stakes, the compost heap, old buckets and so on.

Calculating materials

Save time and money by calculating quantities and ordering in bulk.

Area

Rectangle – *Multiply the length by the breadth to give you the area. A plot 30 × 15 m = 450 square m (100 × 50 ft = 5,000 square ft).*

Circle – *Area of a circle is pi × radius squared, with pi being 3.14. For example, with a 3 m (10 ft) diameter circle the sum is 3.14 × 1.5 squared, meaning 3.14 × 2.25 = c.7 sq m (3.14 × 25 = c.80 sq ft).*

Irregular – *Draw a square grid over the shape. Find the area of a single square. Gauge how many whole squares you have and multiply them by the area of a single square.*

Volume

The volume is the area of the base multiplied by the height. For example, a tank measuring 90 × 90 × 90 cm has a volume of 729,000 cubic cm (3 × 3 × 3 ft = 27 cubic ft).

Turf is sold as regular shapes – usually about 30 cm (12 in) wide by 45 cm (18 in) long

Soil is sold in cubic metres, by the jumbo bag or truckload

Gravel is sold in cubic metres, by the jumbo bag or truckload

Bricks are sold individually or by the thousand

Stone is sold by the piece or in cubic metres

Concrete is sold ready-mixed in cubic metres or by the jumbo bag

---

The best plants for the job

With thousands of plants to choose from, the challenge is to get the right plants to suit your location. See the Plants section of this book on pages 54–77 for some of the best choices in each category.

Trees: Small trees offer good year-round colour and texture – foliage, blossom, fruit and bark (see pages 54–55).

Hedges: Hedges make good boundaries, attract wildlife and add year-round colour and interest (see pages 56–57).

Herbaceous perennials: These are the plants that last a few years before being lifted and divided (see pages 60–61).

Shrubs: Shrubs are ideal for small gardens (see pages 54–55).

Wall shrubs: Wall shrubs are a good option for small courtyard gardens (see pages 56–57).

Climbing plants: Climbers are essential when walls and fences ring your garden (see pages 58–59).

Annuals, biennials and bedding plants: Summer bedding is formed mainly of these plants (see pages 62–65).

Bamboos and grasses: Bamboos and grasses are good when you want plants in small raised borders and containers (see pages 70–71).

Water plants: You will need plants for the margins, for the areas of bog, and for the water area (see pages 68–69).

Other plants: These include rock, scree and desert plants, container plants, herbs, fruit and vegetables (see pages 66–67 and 72–77).

Planning the work

Why do I need to plan?

The key to good garden design is planning. If you want the project to run smoothly, you must work in a carefully thought-out, step-by-step sequence. It is no good simply rushing in and hoping for the best; you must work out the order of tasks to the very last detail. The best method is to start by establishing the boundaries, and then to work in and up, sorting out the tasks in order – ground levels, infrastructures, features, lawns and finally planting.

STEP-BY-STEP ORDER OF WORK

Step 1
Boundaries
Have one last talk with neighbours about precise positions and heights, and then measure out and build the walls and fences.

Step 2
Ground levels
Dig holes for ponds, and generally move the earth around to suit your needs. Be careful not to bury the valuable topsoil. Put in drainage trenches, water pipes and power cables.

Step 3
Primary infrastructures
Build the primary infrastructures – retaining walls, main paths, drive and foundations.

Step 4
Features and detailing
Build the main features – ponds, pools, sheds and patios – and follow up with details such as steps, small paths, gates and edgings for lawns and borders.

Step 5
Lawns
Make sure that the lawn areas are well drained. Level, rake and roll the ground, and then either sow seed or lay turf.

Step 6
Planting
Prepare the borders and the other planting areas, and plant your chosen shrubs, climbers, trees and bedding plants.

EMPLOYING LANDSCAPERS VERSUS DIY

Of course you can call in landscape contractors, but it will be expensive, and worse still you will miss out on all the fun. By far the best all-round option is to do the work yourself. If you follow the DIY route, you can control the costs, make modifications as you go along, get lots of healthy exercise, save on gym fees, take as much time as you want, ask your friends and family to join in the fun – the kids will love digging holes – and, possibly best of all, the workers can have countless barbecue parties.

Step 1 Boundaries

Being mindful that most neighbour disputes are about things like tall hedges and fence posts, carefully identify your boundaries. Tidy up the hedges and/or build secondary fences in front of them. If you are rebuilding a fence or wall, be sure to talk to your neighbours along the way. Replace only short lengths at a time, so that neither you nor your neighbours lose sight of reference markers.

Step 2 Ground levels

You have three choices with a sloping site: you can leave it as a feature, you can build low retaining walls and make a series of terraces, or you can build one or more retaining large walls and level the whole site. Be aware that changing levels will have an impact on your neighbours' drainage. You must not build the earth up against house walls or fences. Dig out ponds and bury pipes and cables.

Step 3
Primary infrastructures

Build up the various primary retaining walls to hold back the earth, and then follow on with walls for raised beds. Make sure that primary retaining walls are broad-based with drainage points and good foundations. Retaining walls higher than about 90 cm (3 ft) will need to be reinforced with iron bars set into the foundations. Build paths and drives, and foundations (for things like sheds, steps, edges of flower borders and lawns, and brick gate posts).

Step 4
Features and detailing

Put in the main features, such as pond liners for sunken ponds. Build walls around raised ponds, lay patios, tidy up paths and erect sheds; then follow up with small details like steps, small paths and edges around ponds and trees. Build brick gateposts, hang gates, erect pergolas and trellis, and put down lawn and border edgings. If you have got to do anything else that involves digging holes or making a mess, now is the time to do it.

Step 5
Lawns

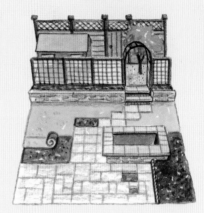

Having seen to it that the lawn areas are well drained – with perforated pipes or trenches filled with rubble – bring back the topsoil and carefully level the ground. Spend time getting it right. Finally roll the ground, and put down seed or lay turf. Keep off the lawn until the ground has settled.

COMMON PROBLEMS AND HOW TO AVOID OR SOLVE THEM

Fence disputes Talk things through with the neighbours at every stage. Leave old posts in place as markers. Leave their fences alone.

Neighbours' trees You cannot do anything about neighbours' trees, other than to trim them from your side. Remember to ask the neighbours if they want the trimmings.

Big rocks Keep rocks as a feature, or get a specialist to remove them.

Clay soil Live with clay soil. Look at neighbouring gardens and see what grows best. For vegetable gardens, make raised borders and buy compost and horse manure – so that you are working above the level of the clay.

Contaminated ground Build over rubble and/or use it as hardcore. If it is something nasty like asbestos or oil, seek specialist advice.

Waterlogged ground Build a pond, lay drainage pipes and create a water garden complete with bog plants.

Unwanted structures Carefully salvage bricks and use them for walls.

Step 6 Planting

Now comes the exciting bit – the planting. Take your time and do your research. You can make considerable cost cuts by phoning around and comparing prices.

• Have a good long look at the finished garden and plan out the planting positions. Prepare the planting areas with just the right soil. Make a plant list.

• Phone up nurseries and garden centres, and generally make enquiries about availability. Make contact with specialist nurseries for items like roses, fruit trees, climbing shrubs, pond plants and fuchsias.

• See if you can cut costs by buying in bulk or by getting all the plants at the same time. Compare prices.

• If you are buying large mature container-grown trees, make sure that there is adequate height and width access.

• If you have doubts about the total planting pattern, start by planting the main feature trees and shrubs.

Tools and materials

What will I need to buy?

Although you can borrow tools and use found, salvaged and gifted materials, such as old bricks and left-over sand, you will inevitably have to buy some new tools and things like cement and wood. Tools and materials come from DIY outlets, builder's merchants and local suppliers. You can make savings in time and energy if you buy the best tools for the task, and in money if you purchase the materials in bulk from local suppliers.

TOOLS

Measuring and marking

You need a basic kit for measuring, marking, checking levels and setting out the site. Spray paint or chalk can be used for marking out straight and curved lines (not illustrated).

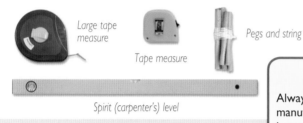

Large tape measure

Tape measure

Pegs and string

Spirit (carpenter's) level

Preparing the site

These tools will enable you to dig, move and level earth. You can hire (rent) a compaction plate (power tamper) for preparing large patio foundations (not illustrated).

Spade

Fork

Shovel

Gloves

Bucket

Sledgehammer

Rake

Wheelbarrow

Brick and stone

This toolkit will allow you to break, chop and cut both stone and brick. You may want to hire (rent) an angle grinder or a cement mixer for big projects.

Club hammer

Masonry drill bit

(Stone) mason's hammer

Bolster (brick) chisel

Bricklayer's (mason's) trowel

Safety

Always follow the manufacturer's instructions. Always protect your eyes, ears and hands when using power tools. Wear a dust mask when using cement powder. Wet cement is corrosive. Always keep children out of harm's way.

Wood

If your designs include fences, gates, pergolas, sheds or decking you are likely to need the tools shown here.

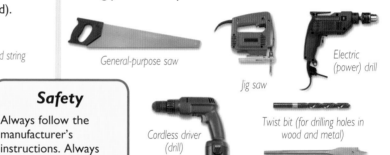

General-purpose saw

Jig saw

Electric (power) drill

Cordless driver (drill)

Twist bit (for drilling holes in wood and metal)

Flat bit (for drilling holes in wood – not for metal)

Gardening

Apart from items like a spade, a fork and a pair of gloves, you may also need a mower and a small number of dedicated tools like those shown below.

Garden shears

Hand fork

Straight-bladed saw

Trowel

Long-handle secateurs

Secateurs

Hoe

MORE TOOLS

Often the best way of getting tools is to buy them when the need arises. For example, you have a spade and fork, but you soon find that you need a shorter, lighter spade, or a fork with a more comfortable handle, so you get another one. If you are less keen on the construction aspects, larger and/or more specific tools like a compaction plate (power tamper) or cement mixer are best borrowed or hired (rented). You could also borrow a few tools, and then buy your own when you know what it is about the borrowed tools that you like.

MATERIALS

Brick and stone

Brick and stone can be purchased direct from the producer, from builder's merchants and from architectural salvage companies.

Concrete paving block

Selection of bricks

Flat stone

Rock

Building stone

Walling blocks

Cobblestones

Decorative gravel

Imitation setts

Artificial stone paver

Border tile

Edging and corner post

Buying earth and turf

Earth is best purchased by the cubic metre or yard in a giant bag or by the truckload. The more you get, the cheaper it will be. Be careful that you do not buy in poorer-quality stuff than you already have.

Turf is sold in rolled-up strips about 30 cm (1 ft) wide and 60–90 cm (2–3 ft) long. The cheapest way is to buy it direct from the grower. They are usually quite happy for you to pick up a small number of strips.

Concrete and mortar

While there are as many 'best' recipes as there are builders, the following work well. The numbers signify the ratio of ingredients (by volume) to each other, measured in the same manner (such as by the shovelful).

Concrete	Mortar
3 aggregate + 2 sand + 1 cement	3 sand + 1 cement

Wood

Wood in all its forms can be obtained variously from timber (lumber) yards, builder's merchants, garden centres and specialist suppliers.

Useful wood sections

Trellis

Bark chippings

Log roll

Sleeper (tie)

Ponds and water features

All the items and materials needed for creating ponds and water features can be obtained from garden centres, water-garden centres and specialist suppliers. For large ponds choose a flexible liner. Geotextile is a soft textile material that is laid underneath flexible pond liners and helps prevent the liner from being damaged by sharp stones. A sump is often used in small water features.

Geotextile and flexible pond linings

Rigid liner (formal shape)   Rigid liner (informal shape)   Plastic sump   Rigid cascade liner

MORE MATERIALS

As garden design is becoming more and more popular, so many materials and products, such as decking, garden shelters, butyl pond liners and concrete sculpture, are being sold by dedicated specialist suppliers. The recent popularity of decking has meant that decking companies and companies only selling decking materials are springing up everywhere. You can make contact via local directories or by the internet; that said, however, one of the pleasures of garden design is travelling around searching out good suppliers.

Marking out the site

Will it work in practice?

At long last, you can don your work clothes and start marking your designs out on the ground. Once the pegs have been banged in and the various curves and lines have been marked out with string, you will have a clearer picture of how it is all going to look. Along the way, you will need to make decisions about such things as levels, where to put the earth, when to start digging holes, how much land to give to lawns, and so on.

USING YOUR MASTER DRAWING

Having drawn up a site plan to show existing features, and then used this to create a master design that shows how you ideally want the garden to be (see pages 10–11), take several photocopies of both plans, and put the originals safely to one side. To transfer the master design to the garden, read off the scale (say one grid square on the plan equals 30 cm or 1 ft on the ground) and work out the actual measurements that will be needed in the garden. Mark out the shapes using pegs and string, sand trickled from a bottle, or a can of spray chalk.

A master plan

Slopes and holes

Assessing the degree of slope: Bang in two pegs, at the highest and lowest points, so that they are flush with the ground. Bridge the pegs with a length of wood and check with a spirit (carpenter's) level.

Levelling a slope: If you do not mind hard work, you can either bring in materials to level up the low ground or dig into the slope and move the soil from the highest to the lowest point.

Easy options with slopes: Incorporate the slopes into your design using steps, terraces and waterfalls; alternatively, build a raised deck that stands above the slope.

Dealing with holes and mounds: Turn holes and mounds into exciting design features such as ponds, bogs and rockeries, or use the earth from the mounds to fill the holes.

Shed or chalet
Make sure, when you set out the size and shape on the ground, that there is room all around for maintenance. Visit the site at various times throughout the day to get a feel of how it is going to be.

All your measurements should relate to one or more fixed points, such as the house, the front gate and mature trees. Start by marking out what you consider is the most important feature – say the path that runs the full length of the garden – and then fill in with the other features. Live with the bare bones of the marked-out design for a day or so to see if it works.

Rockery
It is always a good idea to site the rockery on high ground – it looks more natural and it saves on stone. Make sure that there is easy access for stone delivery.

Patio
Mark out the shape of the patio, and carefully consider how you will level it up. Try it out at various times of the day to see how it fares for sun, shade and shelter.

Flower borders
Transfer irregularly shaped 'boundary' flower borders from the design to the garden by measuring out at regular intervals from the boundary fences and then joining up the resulting points.

Pond
Identify the centre of the pond with a peg, and then mark the edges out from this point. Go for the biggest possible pond, because it will look smaller when it is finished.

Path
Paths are important. Make sure that they are wide enough for things like the wheelbarrow, mower and kids' ride-on toys. Walk the route and live with it for a day or so. Be prepared to change it to suit the needs of the whole household.

Marking out squares and rectangles

Use pegs and string to fix the position of one side. Bang in subsequent pegs to fix a second side in relation to the first, and so on. Use a tape measure to check that opposite sides are equal in length, and parallel. To achieve perfect squareness, measure the diagonals and make small adjustments to the sides until the diagonal measurements are identical.

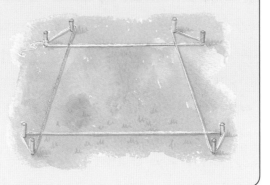

Marking out circles

Make two marks on the ground – one to fix the centre of the circle, and one to fix the most critically placed point on the circumference. Bang a peg in at the centre. Cut a length of string and tie a loop at one end and slip it over the peg. Tie a loop at the other end so that it centres on the critical circumference point. Slide a bottle full of sand, lentils or rice into the loop, and use this to scribe the circle out on the ground.

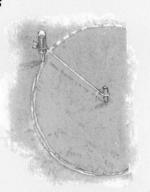

Marking out ellipses

Bang in two pegs to mark out the total length of the ellipse, and one to fix the centre. Bang in two pegs to mark the total width of the ellipse. Tie a length of string to make a loop that tightly encloses the two end pegs, and one or other of the width pegs. Slide a bottle full of sand, lentils or rice into the loop at one or other of the width points, remove the two width pegs, and scribe the ellipse out on the ground.

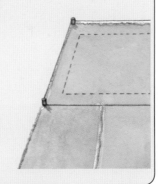

Marking out curves

Take a pile of stones and mark the curve out on the ground. Stand back, look at it from different viewpoints, and make adjustments. Live with the curve for a while. When you are happy with the curve, mark it in with sand or spray chalk and remove the stones.

Remember that long, broad-sweeping curves are generally easier on the eye than small, tight ones.

REMOVING TURF

Use a tape measure, pegs and string to mark the area out on the ground. Use a spade to slice the whole area into a spade-width grid. One square at a time, hold the spade at a low angle and slice under to remove the turf.

MOVING EARTH

As the precious topsoil always needs to finish up on top, start by using a wheelbarrow and spade to put the topsoil safely to one side. Use the subsoil to fill in holes or boggy areas, or to build up banks. Spread the topsoil over the subsoil.

FOUNDATIONS AND DEPTHS

A foundation is a construction below ground that distributes and supports the weight of the structure. The basic rule is the greater the load (the weight and size), the larger the foundation needs to be.

PATIOS

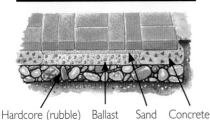

Hardcore (rubble)   Ballast   Sand   Concrete

A basic foundation for a patio that is being built on firm, well-drained ground.

WALLS

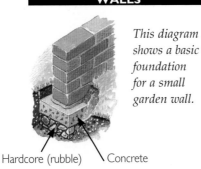

This diagram shows a basic foundation for a small garden wall.

Hardcore (rubble)   Concrete

DIGGERS

A hired (rented) digger will certainly get the job done fast, but will it fit through your gates? Will it damage the drive, lawns, trees and/or shrubs?

FORMWORKS

A formwork is a box-like frame – made from 2.5 cm (1 in) thick planks – that is used on soft ground to hold back the sides of a foundation hole. The formwork can be left in place.

Walls, fences, hedges and gates

Building walls, erecting fences, planting hedges and hanging gates are all little-by-little procedures that involve you doing your best at every stage.

What are the options?

Of course, you might have trouble to start with, but if you follow the directions and remember to take your time, then not only will you end up with a good finished product but you will also have lots of fun along the way. The best advice is to take it slowly – undertake a small project over several days.

BRICK WALLS

There is something very enjoyable about building a simple brick wall – the process of trowelling slices of smooth soft mortar, and placing one brick upon another, is amazingly therapeutic. If you want to enhance your garden with an attractive, traditional, easy-to-use, long-lasting material, then you cannot do better than go for bricks. The procedure involves putting down compacted rubble, laying a slab of concrete over the rubble, and then bedding a pattern of bricks in mortar on top of the concrete. A basic two-brick thick wall is a good choice for most garden walls, but single brick thickness can also work well.

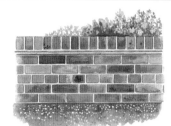
↗ *A low garden wall incorporating a tile and soldier course feature.*

↗ *You will soon get the feel of how to apply the soft mortar with a trowel.*

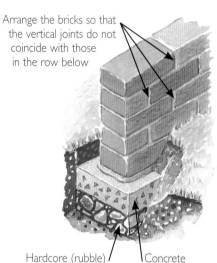
Arrange the bricks so that the vertical joints do not coincide with those in the row below

Hardcore (rubble)　　Concrete

↗ *A low, single-thickness brick wall with a concrete and rubble foundation.*

STONE WALLS

↗ *A mixed-stone wall with feature stones for pots.*

↗ *A stone wall topped with brick can be attractive.*

↗ *A double-thickness stone wall with a planting cavity.*

Dry-stone walls are a good option for gardens – they are easy to build, strong and long-lasting, they can be built without cement or mortar, and of course they are wonderfully attractive. The traditional technique, developed over many thousands of years, involves stacking stone upon stone – with earth and small stones as an infill – so that the resulting wall is broad-based with the sides leaning in. The procedure is to dig out a trench for the foundation, put compacted rubble in the trench, and then start stacking the stones. Stone walls can also be built using mortar, in the same way as for brick walls (see above).

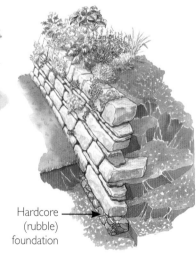
Hardcore (rubble) foundation

↗ *A traditional dry-stone wall can also be used as a retaining wall for a raised bed or border, with plants in the gaps.*

FENCES

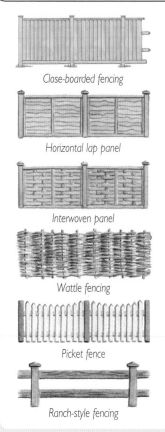

Close-boarded fencing

Horizontal lap panel

Interwoven panel

Wattle fencing

Picket fence

Ranch-style fencing

Wooden fences are a good option. Not only is there a huge selection to choose from, but better still they can be up and running in the space of a weekend. You can have traditional white-painted pickets, trellis, close boards, horizontal lap panels, interwoven panels, woven wattles, ranch-style fences, and so on. You have the choice of self-building or employing a specialist company. If you choose the latter, you need to watch out for poor-quality companies. The best advice is to ask friends and neighbours if they can make recommendations.

Fixing posts

A new wooden post is best set by digging a hole and tamping dirt around it a little at a time until the hole is filled. You could also pour concrete to fill the hole. Metal post supports driven into the ground are often not very sturdy.

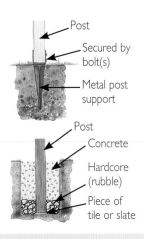

Post

Secured by bolt(s)

Metal post support

Post

Concrete

Hardcore (rubble)

Piece of tile or slate

Fence repairs

Remove the broken panel complete with posts and fixings. Set the new posts in place, standing on rubble in holes. Clamp the panel in place between the posts and make adjustments, with bricks, to bring the panel up to the right height. Finally, top the holes up with concrete. Leave the clamps until the concrete is set.

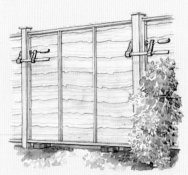

The new panel must be clamped in the correct position until the concrete has set.

HEDGES

Hedges are a great choice for boundaries and decorative features – as long as you have space and time. For example, a boundary hedge might take 4–5 years to grow to a good height, it might need to be about 1.2–1.5 m (4–5 ft) wide at the base, and once grown it will need to be variously clipped and sorted to keep it in good condition. All that said, a good dense hedge will create privacy, provide shelter, reduce nuisance noise and generally hold back dogs, cattle, and unwanted neighbours.

↗ *A crisp, formal hedge consisting of two different foliage colours.*

↙ *Hedges can be shaped to fit in the surrounding landscape, blending with nearby structures or standing out for eye-catching interest.*

GATES AND GATEWAYS

A picket gate can look nicely informal.

Close-boarded gates are good for hedges.

Wrought-iron gates are ideal for front gardens.

Anti-theft gates

With wrought-iron gates, either have tops welded on the hinge pegs, or turn the top peg over so that the gate is captured and cannot easily be lifted off the hinge pegs. Use bolts instead of screws for fixing hinges to wood.

Arched gateways in hedges, ironwork with roses growing over it, iron gates, picket gates, close-boarded gates – there are hundreds of options to choose from. You need to define precisely what you want from a gate. For example, do you want something small, friendly, pretty and decorative, or something large, intimidating, strong and secure?

Patios

Does it have to be paving slabs?

There are hundreds of ways of making patios and many materials to choose from. You could use brick, concrete slab, reconstituted stone, crushed stone, gravel or tree bark. You could have bricks in straight lines, in zigzags, as chevrons or in soldier courses. There are countless options for each material. Look at the materials and forms in your locality – your house, and neighbouring houses, walls and paths – and then do your best to follow on.

A small patio made with found brick blends in perfectly here.

A patio made from a mixture of materials – concrete slabs, found stone and old bricks – looks good in the right setting.

This rather formal stone patio is uplifted by the planting wall.

PATIO OPTIONS

↗ *An existing patio extended with gravel, cobblestones and stepping stones.*

↗ *This patio has been created using a mixture of old bricks, stone and tiles.*

↗ *An unusual patio made from worn slate inside a hexagonal border.*

← *If you want something a bit different, the strong shape of this circle looks great set within lawn and plants.*

← *For a decorative patio, you could try mixing plain setts and cobblestones in a pretty pattern.*

SHAPE, STYLE AND PLACEMENT

Gone are the days when the best you could hope for in patio comfort was eight grey concrete slabs and two old armchairs; now you can have a patio in just about any shape, colour and style that takes your fancy. A patio is now considered to be more an extension of the house than just a level area in the garden. Just as you want to make the best of the various rooms in your house, now you can shape and decorate the patio to suit your desires and needs.

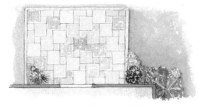

A basic rectangular patio is a good low-cost option for a small garden.

Geometric combinations – circles and rectangles are wonderfully dynamic – can be used to create separate patio 'rooms', with some areas being set at different levels to increase the visual interest.

How to build a brick patio

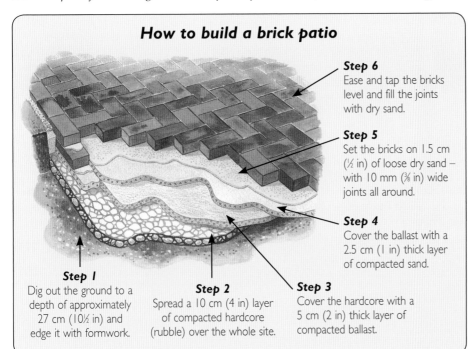

Step 6
Ease and tap the bricks level and fill the joints with dry sand.

Step 5
Set the bricks on 1.5 cm (½ in) of loose dry sand – with 10 mm (⅜ in) wide joints all around.

Step 4
Cover the ballast with a 2.5 cm (1 in) thick layer of compacted sand.

Step 1
Dig out the ground to a depth of approximately 27 cm (10½ in) and edge it with formwork.

Step 2
Spread a 10 cm (4 in) layer of compacted hardcore (rubble) over the whole site.

Step 3
Cover the hardcore with a 5 cm (2 in) thick layer of compacted ballast.

How to build a paving-slab patio

Step 3
Bang 30 cm (1 ft) long wooden pegs in over the site, so that they are level and standing proud by about 15 cm (6 in).

Step 4
Cover the site first with 10 cm (4 in) of compacted hardcore (rubble), then 40 mm (1¾ in) of compacted sand, and lastly 10 mm (⅜ in) of soft sand.

Step 2
Remove the turf and topsoil down to a depth of 20 cm (8 in).

Step 1
Mark out a rectangular area (with 90° corners) using pegs and string.

Step 5
Set the slabs in place and carefully level.

Step 6
Brush fine dry sand into the joints.

DRAINAGE SLOPES

In the context of good drainage, a patio needs either to be exactly level, open-jointed and set on sand, or very slightly sloped. A good angle of slope is a fall of about 3 mm (⅛ in) in every 1 m (3½ ft).

NON-SLIP SURFACES

Old brick, stable pavers – like bricks but with a crisscross pattern – and tamped concrete make relatively good non-slip surfaces, as long as they are dry and kept free from algae.

PATIO ADDITIONS

Pergolas A pergola not only gives a patio architectural form, and provides a framework for climbing plants, it also provides shade.

Water features The sounds of a spouting wall mask or bubbling fountain are very relaxing.

Barbecue Consider building a permanent brick barbecue.

Built-in furniture Bench seats or stone-slab coffee tables save on moving and storing garden furniture.

QUICK PATIO

In the sense that a patio is no more than a well-drained firm area – somewhere to sit and play – a good, swift, low-cost option is to choose a well-placed, slightly sloping area, level it up with a thin layer of ballast, cover it with woven plastic sheet, and then top it off with crushed bark.

Decking

The exciting thing about decking is its immediacy. You might have to mix a small amount of concrete for the footings, but, that apart, you can simply float the deck over the existing garden – over old concrete, damp areas, rocks, slopes – and have it finished in the space of a long weekend. If you want an area for sitting, but do not have time to create a patio, decking is the perfect solution.

Why should I choose decking?

A small area of decking positioned in a sunny spot right outside the back door provides a relaxing place to unwind with a refreshing drink.

Things to consider

Decking is fun to build and just as much fun to use, but only if you spend time designing and planning all the details of the project. Answers to the following questions will show you the way.

• How are you going to use the deck? Do you want it for sunbathing or sitting in the shade?

• Do you want to use the deck for barbecues, or for the kids to play on?

• Do you want the deck to be physically linked in some way to the house or set in isolation?

• Do you want the deck to be raised up on legs or set more or less at ground level?

• If you plan to have a raised deck on unstable ground, will you need the advice of, say, a structural engineer?

• Does the deck need to wrap around the corner of the house like a Japanese *engawa*, or can it run straight out like a pier?

• Do you want a low-cost option, or are you going for the most expensive wood?

• Will your designs in any way affect your neighbours? For example, will a raised deck impinge on their privacy?

• Are there any overhead power lines that are going to be a problem?

• Some areas need planning permission for this kind of work. Will you need planning permission?

DECKING DESIGNS

This stepped decking has an integral bench and railing, together with handy underseat storage space.

Low-level decking is ideal for a pondside patio, and here the established tree will provide welcome shade in summer.

Raised porch decking with a fancy handrail and trellis – the steps also provide a pleasant way to enter the garden.

This large raised deck with steps and handrail is made more private by the addition of the trellis screens.

HOW TO BUILD A RAISED DECK

Dig holes and set posts to follow your local codes. Take extra care to make sure the posts are plumb. Bolt joists that run around the perimeter to the posts, ensuring the joists are perfectly level. Add the interior joists using joist hangers. Cover the joists with decking and then add decorative railings.

↗ *Plan view showing how the underframe supports the decking boards that are laid over the top.*

↖ *A raised deck like this is good for a wild garden where the ground is uneven.*

SPLIT LEVELS

A split-level deck is a good option when you have a slightly sloping site, or when the upper step needs to be raised up above an existing structure – such as an old foundation or underground drain.

MORE OPPORTUNITIES

A deck is just a platform made from wood, so there are lots of interesting options. You could have a decking walkway snaking across the garden, a deck made from railway sleepers (railroad ties), decking steps, a bridge made from decking, a decking-type area around a tree, a series of terrace-like decks running up a slope, a raised deck at the water's edge, and so on.

SLOPES

Overlapping decking is a good solution for a sloping garden. All you do is build a series of decks that raise up and overlap each other like huge steps.

PLANK PATTERNS

Laying the boards in different patterns will add visual interest to the deck.

Angled 45° to the joists

Angle-cut zigzag

Square-cut herringbone

Checkerboard parquet

At right angles to joists

Diamond frame

BALUSTRADE OPTIONS

The design of the balustrade can also transform the appearance of a deck.

Horizontal plain

Vertical traditional

Traditional diamond trellis

Modern square trellis

Modern 'Chinese' trellis

1930s sunburst

DECKING STEPS

Simple three-tread steps are good for a low deck and easy to fix.

Open-plane steps with a fancy fretted balustrade are more complicated but can look stunning.

Codes and deck construction

Although some people consider following codes a hassle, you should remember that codes are developed to make sure your deck is up to the task of holding the weight of people and other items. A casual gathering of six friends could easily add a thousand pounds to the deck, and you want it to be sturdy. Also, if one follows the codes, it is much more likely that your deck will last much longer. Depending on the size of your deck, codes dictate the depth you must sink your support posts, the kinds of hardware you should use to hold it together and even the size of posts, beams, joists and decking. Codes dictate things like the size of gaps that are allowable in the railing to ensure a toddler doesn't topple off the deck. Contact your local building inspector to find out where you can learn about your local codes.

Paths and steps

Much depends upon type and size, but the average traditional red-brick path will probably take 3–5 days to design and create – a day for planning and marking out, and the rest of the time for removing the topsoil and building. A wooden walkway or a path made from gravel or tree bark can usually be put down in the space of a long weekend, but a flight of brick and stone steps might take a week or more, depending on the structure of the subsoil.

PATHS IN THE GARDEN

A simple crushed stone path is just right for this scented garden, and the edges are softened by the spread of the plants.

This path, complete with steps, raised walls and other features has been deliberately designed to make a grand statement.

DESIGNING AND PLANNING PATHS

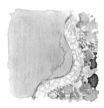

Following the edge of a flower border

What do you want from your path? Do you want it to be the shortest route between two points – such as the swiftest route from the kitchen to the compost heap – or do you want it to be a slow, meandering route that takes in all the best bits of the garden? Do you want the path to be plain and functional – just a concrete strip – or do you want it to be decorative, with lots of colour and different materials?

PATH OPTIONS

Providing a walk around the garden

Leading to a particular feature

Old pieces of stone suit a country garden

Curved paths are good for informal areas

A traditional herringbone brick path

Crazy (cleft stone) paving is suitable for a relaxed garden

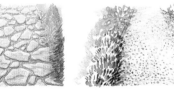

Cobblestone paths are easy to lay

Gravel and lavender are a good mix

Path construction

Gravel A gravel path is a joy – it looks good and is relatively easy to install. Remove the turf and topsoil to a depth of 20 cm (8 in), and then put down a 10 cm (4 in) thick layer of compacted hardcore (rubble) followed by a 10 cm (4 in) layer of pea gravel.

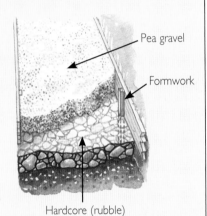

Pea gravel

Formwork

Hardcore (rubble)

Path construction – brick A red-brick path is a good traditional option. Remove the turf and topsoil down to a depth of 20 cm (8 in), and then put down 8 cm (3½ in) of compacted hardcore, 20 mm (⅞ in) of compacted ballast, 20 mm (⅞ in) of compacted sharp sand and 5 mm (¼ in) of soft sand, followed by the bricks.

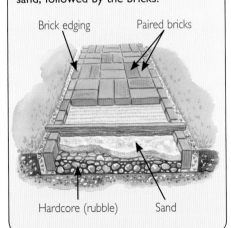

Brick edging

Paired bricks

Hardcore (rubble)

Sand

STEPS IN THE GARDEN

These attractive formal steps have been created with stone slabs forming the treads and bricks forming the risers.

Informal steps made from reclaimed railway sleepers (railroad ties) are excellent for a country garden using natural materials.

These brick and stone steps are adjoined by buttress hand supports, complete with lights for illuminating the steps after dark.

DESIGNING AND PLANNING STEPS

A functional feature

If you have a sloping garden, you have the choice of scrambling about and just hoping that you do not slip, or you can build steps. Apart from being a good, practical solution, steps also function as a decorative feature that leads the eye from one level to another.

Calculations

Good, comfortable steps need to have risers at about 15–18 cm (6–7 in) high, with treads that measure 30–40 cm (12–16 in) from front to back.

Construction and materials

While there are lots of options – brick, stone, sleepers (ties), wood, and many more beside – some materials are easier to use than others. For example, a mix of brick and stone is a good choice – the bricks are just right for the risers, and the stone can easily be sized to suit the depth of the treads.

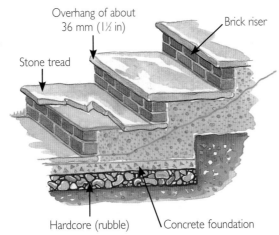

Overhang of about 36 mm (1½ in)
Brick riser
Stone tread
Hardcore (rubble)
Concrete foundation

A flight of steps leading from a path up to a patio. To a great extent, the whole flight is supported on the concrete foundation that runs under the bottom step.

STEP OPTIONS

Log and gravel steps are a good option for a country garden, as they are quick to create.

These corner steps in a path have been made from square paving slabs and bricks.

PATH AND STEP PROBLEM-SOLVING

Soft, sloping ground This flight of brick steps, with concrete over hardcore (rubble) under every tread, is a good option for soft, damp ground. The extra-thick layer of hardcore (rubble) and the pipe under the bottom step help to spread the load and drain off the water.

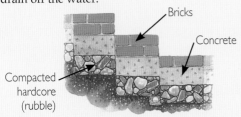

Bricks
Concrete
Compacted hardcore (rubble)

Boggy ground A simple pole walkway is a good option for boggy ground. The poles are supported on posts or piles – the damper the ground, the longer the piles required. If you are worried about slipping, you could also include a handrail, as here.

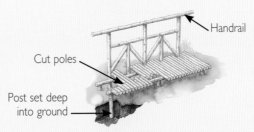

Handrail
Cut poles
Post set deep into ground

Existing concrete steps The best way of sorting out an ugly flight of concrete steps is to cover them with brick. All you do is leave the concrete in place and lay bricks over the treads. The remaining bits of concrete – the risers – can be stained or painted.

Lawns and edgings

Lawns not only help to define and unify spaces, they also lead the eye from one area to another. If you want to increase the apparent size of your garden, run the lawns through and around the beds; if you want to chop the space into 'rooms', have individual areas of lawn. A lawn is a great, low-cost, easy-maintenance, hardwearing but soft, self-renewing, multi-purpose surface for all the family. Remember to choose a grass type to suit your particular needs.

LAWN DESIGN

A lawn can be used for physical activities such as playing games, as a design feature, such as in a formal garden where the lawn is seen as a visual pattern-making device that links beds and paths, or as a functional path-like form that leads from one area of the garden to another. From a practical mowing point of view, the ideal lawn has a smooth-curved outline, with the edge set slightly higher than the surrounds so that the lawnmower can be run over the edge.

PREPARING THE SITE

Dig down to a depth of 7–10 cm (3–4 in). Remove stones and perennial weeds, break up large clods, and pick up debris. On a day when the ground feels dry, rake over the plot. Work systematically and firm the soil with your feet.

Sowing seed

- Buy a seed mixture that suits your needs.
- Pick a day when the soil is dry underfoot – either in the autumn or spring – and go over the whole site gently raking the surface.
- Seeding in fall is the best option largely because grass can continue to grow at slightly lower temperatures than most weeds. So a lawn started in early fall gives the grass an edge over competing plants.
- Kill any existing lawn or weeds with a herbicide recommended by a local garden center or with black plastic sheeting.
- Watering grass seed and newly sprouted grass is critical to its survival and thriving growth.
- Try to stay off of newly sprouted grass and keep pets and children away.

MAINTENANCE

At regular intervals throughout the growing season, you need to mow the lawn, water it in dry spells, trim the edges, aerate with a fork, rake up dead grass, topdress to fill hollows and improve vigour, and brush away worm casts. Things like feeding with fertilizer, killing moss and rolling should only be done if and when the need arises.

Laying turf

- Use string and a couple of pegs to set a straight guideline along one edge of the site.
- Make sure that the weather is going to stay fine, check the size of the turves with the supplier – mostly they measure about 30 cm (1 ft) wide and 90 cm (3 ft) long – and then order slightly more turf than you think you will need.
- Starting from the guideline, lay the first row of turves and gently ease and tamp them into place.
- When you come to the second row, cut the first turf into half and then continue butting the second row hard against the first – so that the end joints are staggered from row to row, like a brick pattern.
- Continue working across the site, standing on a plank on the turf that has just been put down, and always looking towards the next line of turf that needs to be put down.
- When the turf has been down for about a week, use a half-moon edging iron or an old bread knife to trim and shape curved edges.
- Watering newly lain sod is critical to its survival. The deeper roots that grass develops have been cut off, so the grass needs daily watering for several weeks depending on your soil and the weather.

LAWN EDGING OPTIONS

The lawn edging can be anything from a row of bricks hidden away just below the surface of the ground through to a trench full of pea gravel, a nicely cut edge where the lawn meets a flower bed, or a line of fancy tiles set on edge. There are many options.

Wooden boards fixed to pegs

Soldier bricks set on end

Ready-made logroll

Fancy rope-edge tiles

Round-nose tiles on edge

Bricks set at an angle

Borders

In garden design, a border can be regarded both as an area for planting and as a three-dimensional element. Most modern gardens consist of four elements – lawns, paving, borders and water – so borders figure very highly in the scheme of things. When it comes to designing a border, there are three aspects to consider: the shape as seen on the ground, the character of the structure (the edgings, retaining wall and so on) and the type of planting it will support.

How do I design a border?

BORDER DESIGNS IN PLAN VIEW

Informal edge-strip borders

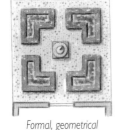
Formal, geometrical borders

Informal island border in lawn

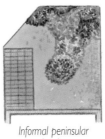
Informal peninsular border

There are only six basic types of border.
- The edge-strip border that uses the boundary fence as a backdrop.
- The geometrical border that relates to some sort of formal design.
- The island border that is set within a sea of lawns.
- The peninsular border that runs out from a boundary fence.
- The border that runs hard up against the wall of the house.
- The border that relates to some sort of functional scheme – it looks to the sun, is just the right width away from the wall for the wheelbarrow, or whatever it might be.

When you come to design a border, you have to decide how you want it to figure in the scheme of things. For example, do you just want to break up an area of lawn, put distance between you and your neighbours, or create the illusion that your garden is, for example, wider or shorter?

PLANTING SCHEMES

(Above) Mixed borders have an exciting, dynamic nature – they are invariably colourful and vibrant.

(Above) A mixed border in summer is usually packed with colour, texture and form. This example includes climbers on tripods, shrubs and herbaceous perennials in a variety of flower colours.

EDGINGS

Edgings function on two levels: they physically prevent the earth of the border running over the path or lawn next to it, and they are a design feature in their own right – such as a wall, a row of tiles or a railway sleeper.

Raised borders

Ready-made rustic log rolls are an easy option.

A double-thickness wall is a good choice for a small garden.

Red brick is a good traditional choice.

MULCH

A mulch has many functions. For example, while a mulch such as a layer of manure or tree bark prevents the soil from drying out, holds back the growth of weeds and rots down to enrich the soil, a mulch such as pea gravel or crushed rock holds in moisture, holds back the weeds and functions as a design feature in its own right.

Pergolas, arches and trellis

If your idea of heaven is a mix of woodwork and gardening, you are going to enjoy building features such as pergolas and arches. Just think about it – a nice bit of woodwork followed by lazing under your beautifully crafted garden pergola, with a drink and a good book just within reach, all perfectly enclosed with an impressive trellis, with fragrant plants and dappled sunlight all around. Pergolas, arches and trellis can all be used to create instant features.

A pergola weighed down with a vine creates an eye-catching feature as well as a very private area.

A ready-made arch is good for creating instant height, but plants will take time to grow over it.

Plant-covered trellis is a good option if you want privacy. Use a variety of different climbers to add interest.

DESIGNING AND PLANNING PERGOLAS

If you want to create an instant architectural feature in your garden – a place to snooze and play in the shade, a structure for growing climbing plants over, and an eye-catching focal point – then a pergola is an exciting option. The visual impact of a pergola clothed with a wisteria, a grapevine or a honeysuckle can be absolutely stunning. If you are wondering if there is enough room in your garden, a pergola can easily be shaped to suit your needs. It can be anything from four uprights topped with a handful of cross-beams – just large enough to sit under – or a lean-to structure made from rustic poles, through to a substantial brick and wooden walkway that runs the length of the garden.

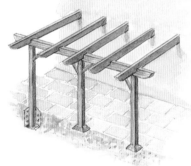

↗ *A lean-to pergola is a traditional option that is a very good choice for a patio area, especially in a small garden.*

↗ *Radial-topped pergolas provide distinctive points of interest.*

↗ *Climbing plants can be used to transform an old, ugly pergola into a striking feature.*

↗ *A traditional pergola bedecked with wisteria is a beautiful, inspiring sight.*

↗ *A porch-type pergola complete with lattice screens.*

↗ *This simple pergola has been constructed using rustic poles.*

ARCHES

Arches are functional in the sense that they can provide a support for plants, and of course they add architectural style, but a small, well-placed arch can also be beckoning and mysterious – an inviting route or gateway for your feet, eyes and mind to pass through. At the practical level, a wooden arch over a gate is a really good way of strengthening and bracing the gateposts. All you do is have posts that are slightly higher than head height, and top them off with a pergola-like cross-beam. If you have plans to create a romantic garden and like the notion of holding hands under a leafy bower, then an arch in a hedge or an arch-like tunnel covered with a scented climber such as a honeysuckle is a good feature to go for.

↗ *This arch-pergola leads the eye to a focal point.*

↗ *Here a flower-covered arch creates a secluded bower.*

↗ *A rose-covered arch is perfect for a country garden.*

↗ *An arch has been used to transform this plain doorway.*

↗ *The trellis arch makes more of this simple door.*

Arches in hedges

↗ *Arches in hedges can be used to create sudden and surprising entrances into other parts of the garden. Unusual shapes will create talking points for visitors, and can be used as design features to complement the overall style of the garden.*

TRELLIS

While, at the practical level, trellis is no more than a structure or pattern of slender wooden strips used for supporting plants – as with free-standing trellis, or a trellis fence, or trellis fixed to the wall of a house – a piece of trellis can also be an imposing and eye-catching architectural feature in its own right. In the 18th and 19th centuries in England and Europe it was a much-favoured way of embellishing the house and garden. One such design involved covering the whole outside of the house with a pattern of trellis, with the effect that the house looked delicate – like wedding-cake decoration. With this in mind, perhaps trelliswork is the answer to the problem of hiding an ugly garage or a neighbour's unsightly concrete wall.

False-perspective trellis

Trellis with 'window'

Open-character screen

Integral seat

Fixing trellis to walls

Drill pilot holes and fix with screws.

Fit the trellis so that it is distanced from the wall.

GREENWOOD TRELLIS

This pretty little trellis feature is characteristic of the spidery rustic woodwork that was favoured in the 19th century by gardeners who were trying to achieve a romantic cottage garden – a mix of an 18th-century French romantic garden and a pastoral sheep-and-shepherdess garden.

Garden buildings and shelters

What are the possibilities?

There is a long tradition of householders making all manner of garden structures from greenhouses, sheds, porches and gazebos to log cabins and summerhouses. If you enjoy basic 'do-it-yourself', are good with a saw, hammer and drill, and are keen and enthusiastic, then there is no reason at all why you cannot build just about any garden shelter that strikes your fancy. Don't forget, however, that the key words here are 'keen' and 'enthusiastic'!

SHEDS

↗ A small, apex-roofed, free-standing shed.

↗ A medium-sized, pent-roofed shed.

↗ This shed has double doors for easy storage.

↗ This small shed will fit snugly into a corner.

Siting a shed

Walk around your garden and try to visualize the perfect setting for a shed. Of course, much depends on what sort of shed you are looking to build, but ideally it needs to be positioned on dry, high ground, in a quiet spot, with the doors and windows looking towards a nice view. If you can imagine yourself sitting in the shed – dry, warm, with no noise, and sheltered – then you will probably have got it just about right.

Shed foundations

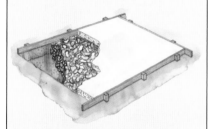

A shed needs to be built on a solid foundation. A good foundation is made up from compacted rubble topped with concrete. Foundations should be built according to your local building code.

GREENHOUSES

Traditional apex design

Modern apex design

Large lean-to

Octagonal design

Mini lean-to

Combination shed/greenhouse

Siting

A greenhouse should be set on dry ground away from anything that is likely to cast shadows or scatter debris, meaning buildings and trees. If you have no choice other than to site it near a fence or a hedge, then try to place it so that it is on the sunny, sheltered side.

Foundations

The average, small, rectangular greenhouse can be set on concrete slabs – one at each corner, with a row of slabs running in through the doorway.

Screening

In mid-summer the interior of a greenhouse can get hot enough to kill the plants within. You can mitigate that heat with automatic vents and by using netting or fabric to create shade.

Mini plastic greenhouses

While a small plastic greenhouse is usually fine for growing a few tomatoes – but even then it can swiftly overheat – it is not a very attractive option from a design point of view.

Barn design formed of sheet glass.

Modern design made of plastic sheeting.

Cloches

Traditional bell jar design made out of blown glass.

SUMMERHOUSES

Siting

A summerhouse can be a magical place – for children sleeping over, for a quiet drink, or for a doze and a read – if it is well sited. It needs to be positioned on dry ground, away from dank corners, with the doors and windows facing the afternoon sun.

➜ *Summerhouses can introduce an upmarket quality and are good for storage and leisure.*

⬅ *Summerhouses can also double up as play rooms for children.*

➜ *A large summer-house can be used as an occasional guest room.*

⬅ *A large summerhouse with insulated walls can be used as a garden office.*

Foundations

Ideally, the summerhouse needs a firm, dry foundation. The best option is to lay a slab of concrete underneath, and then to set the summerhouse up on pressure-treated joists.

ARBOURS

Siting

In the sense that an arbour is designed to be an eye-catching feature, it needs to be sited where it fits into your overall scheme of things – for example, in a corner with climbing plants scrambling over it, or looking out over a pond. If you know that you are most likely to use the arbour in the late afternoon, make sure it takes best advantage of the sun at that time.

↗ *A traditional arbour complete with trellis sides and back and roses growing over it to provide colour and scent.*

Foundations

Although much depends on the design of your particular arbour, just make sure that its base is high and dry. Foundations made from wooden lumber (posts, beams or joists) should be made from lumber that has been treated with a preservative that is designed for 'ground contact'.

PLAY HOUSES

While a play house needs to be sited on dry ground, away from dank corners, and in the sun – just as with a summerhouse – it also needs to be near the house and in full view. It is vital that you can see and hear the children at play. Better yet, join the fun and take part in their imaginative play.

Kids will enjoy the exciting bright colors.

A 'Wendy' house gets its name from the Peter Pan story.

Traditional cottage kitchen garden

A cottage kitchen garden is a romantic coming-together of traditional ideas and notions that have their roots in the agricultural, pre-industrial past when subsistence gardens were made up of vegetable beds, chicken runs, apple trees and compost heaps, with lots of meandering paths, herbs and wild flowers all included in the mix. If you include a lovers' bower, a kissing gate, a water trough or well, or a natural pond, you will be heading in the right direction.

What elements should be included?

A meandering cottage kitchen garden, consisting of a rich mix of flowers and vegetables, can be a visual delight in summer.

Every cottage garden needs a water pump barrel feature.

Plant fruit, vegetables amd flowering plants together for the perfect cottage garden – then both enjoy the flowers and eat the produce.

LOOKING AT THE PROJECT

If we take it that our cottage kitchen garden design (see opposite) draws its inspiration from the small, higgledy-piggledy and somewhat humble country cottages that were once commonplace in England, for example, it will help if your garden is already small with lots of salvaged materials and meandering paths. Have a look at your space and make decisions about what to keep. A good overall size is about 30 m (100 ft) long and 10.5 m (35 ft) wide.

CONSIDERING THE IMPLICATIONS

Traditional cottage kitchen gardens could be described as a bit 'folksy'. Will this 'needs-must-and-mend' mix of fantasy and function suit all the members of your household?

VARIATIONS TO CONSIDER

If you like the overall notion of a loosely defined mix of fruit, vegetables and flowers, but want to nudge the emphasis so there are more vegetables than flowers, or vice versa, then just go your own way.

Design guidelines for success

- A small garden at about 30 x 10.5 m (100 x 35 ft) is ideal.
- Keep the lawn as small as possible.
- Give half of the total space over to the fruit and vegetables.
- Mix the fruit, vegetables and flowers.
- Include meandering paths.
- Use natural materials – best if they are salvaged.
- Use local materials.
- Stay away from modern paints – no blues.
- Try to have a feature like a well or an oak water-butt.
- Use traditional cottage flowers – no exotics.
- Include a pond if there is space – otherwise have a well.
- Include apple and plum trees.

HOW TO CREATE A TRADITIONAL COTTAGE KITCHEN GARDEN

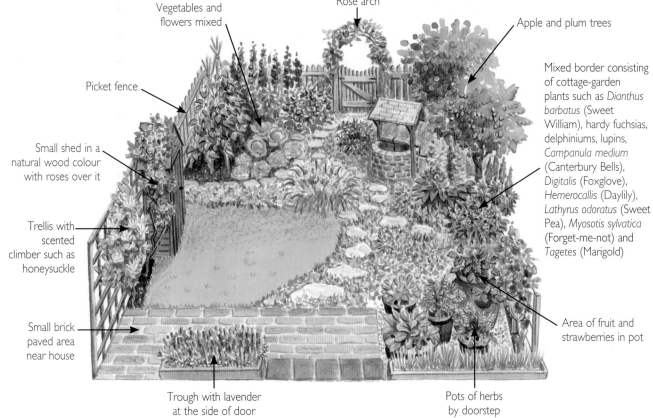

Vegetables and flowers mixed

Rose arch

Apple and plum trees

Picket fence

Small shed in a natural wood colour with roses over it

Trellis with scented climber such as honeysuckle

Small brick paved area near house

Trough with lavender at the side of door

Pots of herbs by doorstep

Mixed border consisting of cottage-garden plants such as *Dianthus barbatus* (Sweet William), hardy fuchsias, delphiniums, lupins, *Campanula medium* (Canterbury Bells), *Digitalis* (Foxglove), *Hemerocallis* (Daylily), *Lathyrus odoratus* (Sweet Pea), *Myosotis sylvatica* (Forget-me-not) and *Tagetes* (Marigold)

Area of fruit and strawberries in pot

Order of work

- Draw up your designs so that they take into account the house, the boundaries, immovable structures and large trees.
- Keep choice plants – either leave them in place or move them to other sites within the garden – and give unwanted plants away or dispose of them.
- Build structures like the pond.
- Put down the paths, and prepare the soil for the various beds.

Planting

Start by making sure that all your existing plants are thriving. Don't be in too much of a hurry with the new planting, other than to set out new shrubs and trees. Plant all the other flowers, herbs, fruit and vegetables in the appropriate seasons.

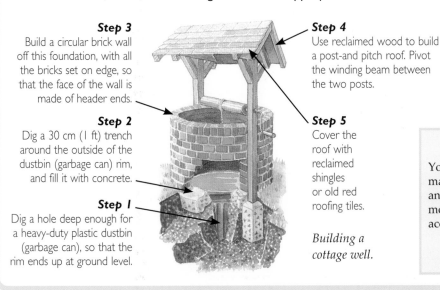

Step 3
Build a circular brick wall off this foundation, with all the bricks set on edge, so that the face of the wall is made of header ends.

Step 2
Dig a 30 cm (1 ft) trench around the outside of the dustbin (garbage can) rim, and fill it with concrete.

Step 1
Dig a hole deep enough for a heavy-duty plastic dustbin (garbage can), so that the rim ends up at ground level.

Step 4
Use reclaimed wood to build a post-and pitch roof. Pivot the winding beam between the two posts.

Step 5
Cover the roof with reclaimed shingles or old red roofing tiles.

Building a cottage well.

Care and maintenance

A good cottage kitchen garden is never tidy or finished, but always in a busy, continuous state of change. The vegetable beds are always going to look scruffy – because you will either be harvesting or preparing for the next crop – and the flowers will always be coming in or going out of season.

DEVELOPMENT

You will find that you are constantly making modifications. One moment such and such a bed will be right, and the next moment you may need to reshape it to accommodate another shrub, for example.

Water garden

How can I incorporate water?

Water gardening provides countless opportunities for the garden designer – all of them exciting. Themes for water gardens include modern city, Japanese, lakeside, forest, formal, seaside and many more. Alternatively, you could choose a style that has its roots in historic buildings, canals, climate, materials, planting or colour, for example. Having a water garden, however large or small, will also enable you to grow some different and fascinating plants.

This formal pond has been designed as part of a large brick patio, with container plants all around it creating instant interest.

If you have a very large garden, you could include a 'natural' pond, surrounded by a wildflower area, that will attract wildlife.

Marginal plants add character to this 'lakeside' pond, providing height, texture and colour as well as shelter for wildlife.

Design guidelines for success

- A medium-sized garden, about 30 × 15 m (100 × 50 ft), is ideal.

- The brick patio needs to take best advantage of sun, shade and shelter.

- The paths must be both functional and decorative – strong and wide enough to take the barrow and the mower, and good on the eye.

- The wild pond needs to be as large as possible.

- Include a lush abundance of plants, so that the pond and the bog garden are seen as one element.

- The rockery needs to be on high ground.

- Include a formal water feature somewhere on the patio.

- The patio needs to be embellished with sweet-smelling climbing plants.

- Plant a lawn in the rest of the garden.

- Include trees and shrubs as a backdrop.

LOOKING AT THE PROJECT

If you look at the design opposite, you will see that there are four basic elements: a wild pond, a bog garden fed by the rainwater run-off from the pond, a large patio that looks down over both the pond and the bog garden, and a formal spouting mask feature on the patio. The whole area is set against a backdrop of trees. Look at your space and make modifications to suit.

CONSIDERING THE IMPLICATIONS

Consider how the design works for you. If you want to have the wild pond slightly bigger and the patio smaller, or the whole design bigger and more formal, then that is fine.

VARIATIONS TO CONSIDER

If you like the overall design but are not so keen on the bog garden, you could have a cascade running off from the main pond into a secondary, smaller, sump pond. Alternatively, you could have small, self-contained bog gardens.

A small, self-contained bog garden with its own water-feed pipe that will keep the soil moist at all times.

This ornate water-spout feature would suit a traditional patio or courtyard area. It can be fixed to stone, brick or block walls.

HOW TO CREATE A WATER GARDEN

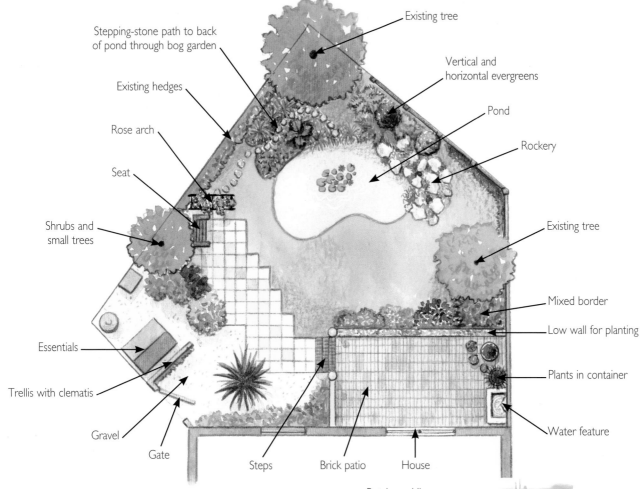

Stepping-stone path to back of pond through bog garden

Existing hedges

Rose arch

Seat

Shrubs and small trees

Essentials

Trellis with clematis

Gravel

Gate

Steps

Brick patio

House

Existing tree

Vertical and horizontal evergreens

Pond

Rockery

Existing tree

Mixed border

Low wall for planting

Plants in container

Water feature

Order of work

- Draw up your designs so that they take into account the house, the boundaries, immovable structures and any large trees.
- Keep choice plants – either leave them in place or move them to other sites within the garden – and give unwanted plants away or dispose of them.
- Dig out the pond and the bog garden, and put the topsoil on one side. Use the subsoil to build up the patio area.
- Build the brick patio and retaining double-wall beds.
- Build the pergola and the patio water feature.
- Build the mini-wall around the pond, lay the butyl liner, and use the scraps of butyl left over from the pond to line the bog garden.
- Use the topsoil to model the edges of the pond and to fill the bog garden.
- Complete the rockery.

Planting

Make sure your existing plants are thriving. Work from the centre to the sides when planting the pond and the bog garden. Plant the lawn. Plant the vines, shrubs and trees, and the flowers, in the appropriate seasons.

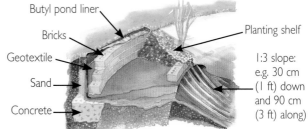

Butyl pond liner

Bricks

Geotextile

Sand

Concrete

Planting shelf

1:3 slope: e.g. 30 cm (1 ft) down and 90 cm (3 ft) along)

Cross-section detail of a pond, showing how all the construction elements fit together to create a successful feature.

Care and maintenance

Other than removing leaves and sludge, and dividing up plants, a good wild pond will, to a great extent, look after itself. You will have to clean it up about once a year.

DEVELOPMENT

A wild pond will always be evolving. As the marginal plants grow, the pond area will appear to get smaller. Within two years, there will probably be frogs, toads, snakes, newts, more birds, and many other creatures – all attracted by the pond.

Modern Mediterranean garden

What is a Mediterranean garden?

A Mediterranean garden is a mixture of different styles that evoke memories of Mediterranean holidays. There are glazed, tiled patios with pools that feel slightly Spanish, terracotta tiles, pottery and statuary fountains that are sort of Italian, enclosed courtyards that look a bit Moroccan, and so on. The overall feeling is one of bright sunlight and colour – flat, rendered walls painted in white, blue, or orange – with dry-climate plants, and crystal-clear water.

Choose a combination of plants and containers that suggest a warm climate through shape and colour.

In this garden, the Moorish arch, the tiles and the palms speak immediately of North Africa or southern Spain.

LOOKING AT THE PROJECT

The design opposite is based on a small courtyard garden. There is a back door leading to a yard, high walls at the sides, and steps leading up or down to a patch of lawn (not shown here), with the total space measuring about 6 m (20 ft) wide and 15 m (50 ft) long. There are four elements: a small, circular, raised pond with a mosaic design and a fountain, a level paved area, rendered walls that have been painted a restful blue, and lots of plants in containers.

CONSIDERING THE IMPLICATIONS

The success of a garden of this character hinges on everything being cool and unruffled – no children's toys, bicycles or dustbins (garbage cans) on view. Is this going to work for you? A garden of this character must be kept clean and tidy.

VARIATIONS TO CONSIDER

If you have in mind a more modern, minimalist garden, you can leave out the pots and the colour – the paint and mosaics – and opt for white ceramic pots and white paint instead.

A Mediterranean-style garden can be created just about anywhere merely by growing the right type of plants.

DESIGN GUIDELINES FOR SUCCESS

- You need a medium-sized yard, about 6 x 15 m (20 x 50 ft).

- You need high walls at the sides.

- All walls should be rendered – there should be no large areas of red brick.

- Walls must be painted flat white, or in a colour like blue or orange ochre.

- You could top the walls off with Spanish-style clay tiles.

- The pond should be raised and either round or square, made from decorative brick or tiles.

- You need lots of terracotta pots or simple raised borders.

- Include lots of easy-care plants, such as yuccas, palms and bamboos.

- Choose good-quality designer furniture – no deck chairs or plastic fold-up chairs.

HOW TO CREATE A MEDITERRANEAN GARDEN

Pots hung on wall brackets

Terracotta tile capping to wall

Tile picture

Circular raised pond and fountain

Pots and plants on steps

Level paved area

Brightly painted door

Fig tree

Pelargoniums in pots

Yucca

Echinops ritro (Globe Thistle)

Sedum (Stonecrop)

Large terracotta pots with palms and grasses

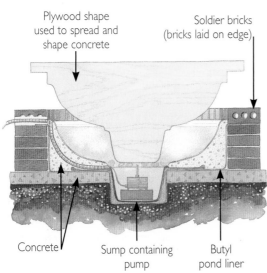

Plywood shape used to spread and shape concrete

Soldier bricks (bricks laid on edge)

Concrete

Sump containing pump

Butyl pond liner

Cross-section detail showing how to make a small circular concrete and brick pond.

Order of work

- Draw up your designs so that they take into account the house, the boundaries, immovable structures, drains and large trees.
- Keep choice plants – either leave them in place or move them to other sites within the garden – and give unwanted plants away or dispose of them.
- Render all the side walls, and paint them the colour of your choice – white, orange ochre or pale blue.
- Pave the yard with tiles – either terracotta or matt white.
- Build the raised pond and decorate the inside and/or the outside with a mosaic design.
- Fit a pump with a simple fountain spray.
- Get as many large terracotta pots as you can afford.

Planting

Make sure your existing plants are thriving. Plant out the containers with dry-garden plants such as *Agave* (Century Plant), *Cortaderia* (Pampas Grass), *Sedum* (Stonecrop), *Eryngium* (Sea Holly) and *Echinops* (Globe Thistle). Spread a mulch consisting of crushed stone or pebbles over the soil.

Care and maintenance

Mediterranean gardens need to be kept clean. At the beginning and end of each season, clean up dead leaves, remove damp mould and renew paintwork.

Development

You could gradually make the garden your own by collecting authentic pottery and tiles and incorporating them. You could add uplighters and a small, discreet barbecue for evening entertaining.

Formal English garden

The term 'formal English garden' has come to describe a rather restrained garden, one with such features as a small, formal pond, steps, dwarf box hedges, a knot garden, a lawn, a pergola, a terrace, red-brick paths, roses and trelliswork. The emphasis should be on small and symmetrical, with the total form drawing inspiration from the late English Tudor period. The key words are English, red bricks, roses and symmetrical.

What does this style entail?

The red bricks, pergola and close-cropped lawns speak of England.

It has been said that English gardeners are obsessed by symmetry, and perhaps the formal English garden bears out this theory.

LOOKING AT THE PROJECT

This design can be modified to suit the size of your garden. There are six primary elements: a level area close to the house, steps leading up or down to the garden, a centrally placed red-brick path, a symmetrical, knot-inspired formation of beds and lawns, dwarf *Buxus sempervirens* (Box) hedges, and lots of roses. While you might not want, or be able, to include all these elements, you do need to keep the knot-like design, the symmetry, the red bricks and the roses.

CONSIDERING THE IMPLICATIONS

There is a lot of work in a garden of this character – topiary hedges to trim, roses to prune and so on. Will this fit into your lifestyle?

VARIATIONS TO CONSIDER

If you have a very small garden, you can create the effect of an English garden by having decorative red-brick paths set within a simple pattern of lawns and beds.

Design guidelines for success

- You need a medium space about 15 m (50 ft) wide and 30 m (100 ft) long.

- The overall design must be symmetrical and geometrical, with the central circle cutting into the lawns.

- You need to have a red-brick path running centrally down the length of the garden.

- You need crisp-edged lawns and flower beds, all mirror-imaged on each side of the main path.

- There should be a pond, flower bed or sculpture right at the centre of the design.

- While the ideal is to have hedges all around, you might have to start off by having fence panels covered with climbing plants.

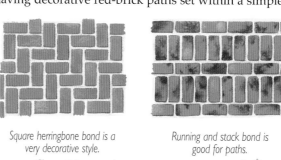

Square herringbone bond is a very decorative style.

Running and stack bond is good for paths.

Double basket weave minimizes the need to cut bricks.

The quintessential English garden look – a red brick path, a rose-covered pergola, low box hedging and a formal seat as a focal point.

HOW TO CREATE A FORMAL ENGLISH GARDEN

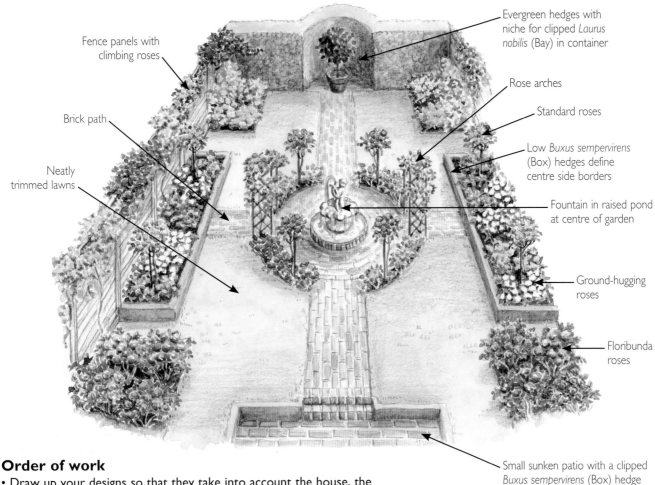

Fence panels with climbing roses

Brick path

Neatly trimmed lawns

Evergreen hedges with niche for clipped *Laurus nobilis* (Bay) in container

Rose arches

Standard roses

Low *Buxus sempervirens* (Box) hedges define centre side borders

Fountain in raised pond at centre of garden

Ground-hugging roses

Floribunda roses

Small sunken patio with a clipped *Buxus sempervirens* (Box) hedge and steps to brick path

Order of work

- Draw up your designs so that they take into account the house, the boundaries, immovable structures and large trees.
- Keep any choice plants – either leave them in place or move them to other sites within the garden – and give unwanted plants away or dispose of them.
- Level the space.
- Use a tape measure, pegs and string to mark out the size and shape of the pond, paths, beds and lawns.
- Build the pond.
- Build the red-brick paths and lay the turf.

Planting

Make sure your existing plants are thriving. Plant out the various roses – ramblers, climbing roses, dwarf or bush roses, standards and shrubs. Plant the *Buxus sempervirens* (Box) hedging and the main *Ligustrum* (Privet) hedging. Set out all the other flowers in the appropriate seasons.

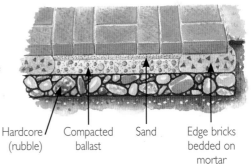

Hardcore (rubble)   Compacted ballast   Sand   Edge bricks bedded on mortar

Cross-section detail showing foundations for a brick patio or path.

Care and maintenance

A formal garden of this character involves a lot of care and maintenance. It does not look too difficult on the face of it – straight lines and unchanging patterns of planting – but of course the unchanging character can only be achieved by hard work. Lawns need to be cut and rolled, the roses are a lifetime's work, and care of the hedges is ongoing.

Development

Wait until the main structure is in place, and then build the other items little by little – things like a pergola, a terrace and a herb garden.

Secluded city garden

How can I get some privacy?

Nobody likes to be overlooked by neighbours when they are trying to relax in the garden, whatever its size. Seclusion is not about how much space you have got, but about being private. It could be a whole garden, or just a little hideaway in a corner of a large garden. The main thing is to create an area that is screened off with walls or fences, shrubs, climbing plants and small trees.

(Above) Rooftop garden with grasses, palms and bamboos growing in decorative containers.

(Left) A private arbour with sweetly scented climbers, lavender and other herbs all around to provide calming fragrance.

Packing the space full of container plants will help create an oasis of seclusion and quiet, as the foliage and flowers will muffle any unwanted sounds.

LOOKING AT THE PROJECT

This design is for a very small city garden, not much more than 6 m (20 ft) wide and 9 m (30 ft) long. It is, in effect, just an area of ground with high walls all around. The garden is composed of four elements: a patch of lawn as you step out of the house, a small gravel area just big enough for a seat or table, a minute pool, and a pitched-roof pergola with an unrestrained jungle of climbing plants growing over it.

CONSIDERING THE IMPLICATIONS

The pergola with the climbing plants will drip during and after rain. Do you want to replace it with, say, a shed with an old armchair, so that you can enjoy the seclusion even when it is raining?

VARIATIONS TO CONSIDER

While this hideaway is made from a pergola with climbing plants on it, you could have anything that takes your fancy – a hut, a huge sun umbrella, an awning. Style it to suit your activities.

Design guidelines for success

- You need a yard at about 6 x 9 m (20 x 30 ft).

- You need high walls on three sides.

- All walls should be left in their rough, as-found state.

- If the walls are rendered, cover them with trellis.

- The pool should be silent – just a pool with fish and plants.

- You need lots of terracotta pots.

- You need lots of climbing plants such as *Vitis vinifera* (Grapevine), *Clematis*, *Passiflora* (Passionflower), *Wisteria* – no roses or plants with thorns or unpleasant smells.

HOW TO CREATE A SECLUDED GARDEN

Blue-painted pergola with a pitched roof

Humulus lupulus 'Aureus' (Golden Hop)

Lonicera periclymenum 'Serotina' (Honeysuckle)

Melianthus major (Honey Bush)

Jasminum officinale (Jasmine)

Iris pseudacorus

Brick-edged gravel

Brick-edged sunken pond

Choisya ternata

Hosta in a terracotta pot

Order of work

- Draw up your designs so that they take into account the house, the boundaries, immovable structures and large trees.
- Keep choice plants – either leave them in place or move them to other sites within the garden – and give unwanted plants away or dispose of them.
- If necessary, build the walls higher.
- Build the pergola.
- Build the pond.
- Pave the yard with a mix of gravel and salvaged bricks.
- Prepare the small beds at the side.

Planting

Make sure your existing plants are thriving. Plant climbers like *Clematis*, *Vitis* (Grapevines), *Humulus* (Hops), *Passiflora* (Passionflower), *Fallopia baldschuanica* (Mile-a-minute Vine), *Lonicera* (Honeysuckle) and *Wisteria*. Spread a mulch of pea gravel or bark over the soil.

Bricks laid on edge are bedded in mortar

Brick or gravel patio

Rigid liner

Concrete under-edging

Sand to support the sides of the liner

Concrete under the planting shelf

Concrete slab foundation

↗ *A circular pond set within a brick or gravel patio. It is level with the ground (sunken) and has a surround of bricks set on edge.*

Care and maintenance

At the beginning and end of each growing season, you need to sweep up dead leaves, clean out the pond and remove debris. Check that your hideaway – shed, shelter or pergola – is in good order.

Development

You could add more plants and modify the structure as you go along. You could have a plastic roof hidden away between the plants and the pergola, so you do not get dripped on.

Japanese garden

Agood part of the Japanese tradition has to do with smallness, privacy and silence. Japanese gardeners have formalized what is needed in the way of elements, features and plants. You should try to include in your design some of the following: a small water feature, stepping stones, boulders, raked gravel, Japanese stone lantern, a small *Acer* (Japanese Maple), a dwarf pine and perhaps a bamboo. Stay away from paint, stained wood and brightly coloured pots.

LOOKING AT THE PROJECT

This design is for a very small yard, with green foliage plants as a backdrop – bamboos and *Acers* and dwarf pines – and includes a stone lantern, boulders and rocks, stepping stones, raked gravel and a deer scarer – a decorative Japanese bamboo water feature.

A traditional Japanese garden with Acers, *feature rocks and raked pea gravel.*

CONSIDERING THE IMPLICATIONS

Will a cool, calm, quiet, unchanging Japanese garden suit the rest of the family? Will you perhaps need additional areas for the children to play in?

VARIATIONS TO CONSIDER

While this design features a deer scarer, you might prefer to go for something a bit more statuesque, such as a Japanese stone basin, which looks a bit like a bird bath.

Design guidelines for success

- You need a yard about 6 x 6 m (20 x 20 ft).
- You need trees, fences or walls at the sides.
- You need a stone basin to catch rainwater, or perhaps a deer scarer.
- You need one or more green or attractive plants in containers – bamboos, dwarf pines and grasses.
- If there is room, include a small tree, something like a small *Acer* (Japanese Maple). Note that the *Acer* will eventually need to be root-pruned to stop it growing into a full-sized tree.
- You need raked gravel.
- You need a stone lantern.
- You need selected pieces of feature stone and stepping stones.

HOW TO CREATE A JAPANESE GARDEN

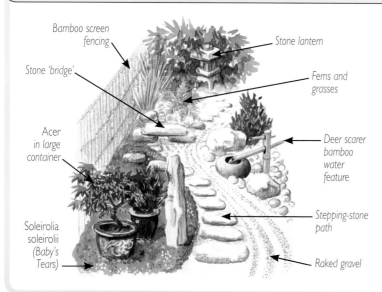

Bamboo screen fencing

Stone 'bridge'

Acer in large container

Soleirolia soleirolii (Baby's Tears)

Stone lantern

Ferns and grasses

Deer scarer bamboo water feature

Stepping-stone path

Raked gravel

Order of work

- Draw up your designs so that they take into account the house, the boundaries, immovable structures and large trees.
- Put plants that you want to save to one side.
- Carefully arrange the lantern.
- Position the deer scarer.
- Arrange the feature stones for best effect.
- Arrange the stepping stones.
- Spread and rake the gravel around the various different features.

Planting

Plant *Acers*, bamboos and dwarf pines in decorative containers. Plant *Soleirolia soleirolii* (Baby's Tears) to spread over the ground.

Wild meadow orchard garden

This garden draws inspiration from the traditional orchard. The important ingredients are standard or half-standard apple and plum trees (Cox and Bramley apples, and Victoria plums), long meadow grass that is scythed twice a year, wild meadow flowers, perhaps a fallen tree and a pile of hay, and maybe a small, natural pond, all ringed with a hawthorn hedge interwoven with wild woodbine. If you can have chickens and geese, so much the better.

How do I create this style?

LOOKING AT THE PROJECT

The design involves a garden as big as you like, planted out with fruit trees and meadow flowers, with hedges all around, and a natural pond if there is enough room. The paths and level areas are mown at regular intervals.

CONSIDERING THE IMPLICATIONS

Will the notion that your garden is wild upset your neighbours?

VARIATIONS TO CONSIDER

You could simplify the design by replacing the mown paths with woodchip or bracken.

All you need for this style of garden is an area of meadow and a few apple trees.

An old orchard makes a perfect patio – the table is ideal for informal meals.

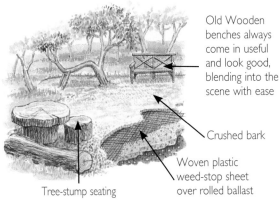

Old Wooden benches always come in useful and look good, blending into the scene with ease

Crushed bark

Woven plastic weed-stop sheet over rolled ballast

Tree-stump seating

Design guidelines for success

- You need a space that is no smaller than 9 m (30 ft) wide and 15 m (50 ft) long.

- You need apple or plum trees – half-standards for a big garden, bush apples for a small space.

- You need hedges or rustic fences all around.

- Shape the pond to suit your space.

- Try to include a selection of 'found' items like logs and tree stumps.

HOW TO CREATE AN ORCHARD MEADOW GARDEN

Order of work
- Draw up your designs so that they take into account the house, the boundaries, immovable structures and large trees.
- Keep choice plants.
- Dig a pond and fit a butyl liner.
- Plant a hedge of *Crataegus monogyna* (Common Hawthorn) all around.

Planting
Plant choice plum and apple trees. Plant the whole area with meadow grass and wildflowers. Mow paths through the grass. Plant the pond with native wild species.

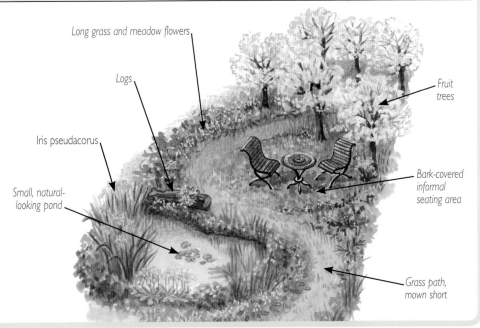

Long grass and meadow flowers

Logs

Iris pseudacorus

Small, natural-looking pond

Fruit trees

Bark-covered informal seating area

Grass path, mown short

Herb garden

What are the options?

Herb gardens come in many forms. You could have a courtyard garden dedicated to growing herbs, herbs in containers placed within a dry garden, herbs as the main planting in and around a patio, herbs grown within the vegetable garden, or an old-fashioned cottage garden planted with herbs – no grass, just lots of little meandering paths with herbs growing in the borders. Some people favour herbs in containers, arranged just outside the back door.

Herbs arranged by the patio, so that they can be easily appreciated.

Herbs in containers not only look good, but can be sited in the best practical position.

LOOKING AT THE PROJECT

In this design, the space – about 2 m (6 ft) from front to back and 2.5–2.7 m (8–9 ft) in width – is completely given over to a cottage herb garden, meaning that the herbs are all suitable for the kitchen. All you have, in effect, is a deep bed edged with red brick, with a brick wall as a backdrop, to keep off cold winds.

CONSIDERING THE IMPLICATIONS

Because beginners are sometimes worried about using unsuitable herbs – perhaps even herbs that are potentially dangerous – this garden only features culinary herbs. Everything can be safely used in the kitchen. If you have doubts, question your supplier.

VARIATIONS TO CONSIDER

This design can easily be modified to suit your garden. It can be stretched in length, mirror-imaged either side of a central path, changed into a raised border, or set within a pattern of lawns and paths – there are countless options.

Design guidelines for success

- You need a space no smaller than about 2 m (6 ft) deep and 2.7 m (9 ft) wide, with a wall as a backdrop.

- Edge the border with bricks.

- The wall needs to be on the cold side, so that the border is facing the sun.

- Arrange the plants so that the tall ones are at the back.

HOW TO CREATE A COTTAGE HERB GARDEN

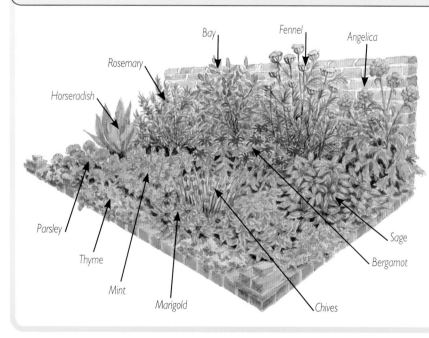

Bay · Fennel · Angelica · Rosemary · Horseradish · Parsley · Thyme · Mint · Marigold · Chives · Bergamot · Sage

Order of work

- Draw up your designs so that they take into account the house, the boundaries, drains, immovable structures and large trees.
- Choose an area in full sun, with a wall on the windward side.
- Mark out the area.
- Double-dig the area to a depth of 30–45 cm (12–18 in).
- Set the brick edging in concrete.
- Improve the soil with an abundance of well-rotted compost and leafmould.

Planting

Container-grown plants can be planted at any time that suits. Sow or plant new herbs in the spring. Work from the back of the bed to the front. Make sure you can reach the plants.

Wildlife garden

All you need is a small patch of water for toads, frogs, newts and fish, nesting-boxes and pole-houses for birds, piles of mossy logs and leaf litter for bugs, and a carefully considered mix of just the right plants. The real fun starts when small birds come in for the bugs, the pond life starts emerging, reptiles come in for the pond life, and bigger birds and mammals come in for the reptiles. Children, cats and dogs all like wildlife gardens.

How can I attract wildlife?

LOOKING AT THE PROJECT

In this design, the space is about 15 m (50 ft) wide and 30 m (100 ft) long. The design is based on a woodland glade. Just imagine that you are walking through a wood and you come across the perfect picnic area. There is a pond, a broad, meandering path of close-cropped grass running down the centre of the plot, woodland trees with shrubs underneath them at the sides, and fallen wood or piles of logs left to rot and decay.

CONSIDERING THE IMPLICATIONS

By the very nature of things, this is going to be a shady garden with lots of leaves and bits and pieces underfoot. It is a good idea to be aware from the start that a wildlife garden is not necessarily a comfortable garden – you will have birds, but they will be coming in for 'unpleasant' things like gnats and bugs.

Colour- and size-dominant plants will always help to frame a garden pond.

VARIATIONS TO CONSIDER

If you like the overall notion of the design but do not want the grass, you could replace it with thick mulch of woodchip and leafmould.

Design guidelines for success

- You need a space no smaller than about 15 m (50 ft) wide and 30 m (100 ft) long. A square plot is better than a long, thin one.

- Include a pond, pool or stream.

- You need a glade of grass or woodchip with trees around it.

- A seat is essential.

- Include one or more bird tables and houses.

- You need trees as a backdrop.

- Plant some shrubs underneath the trees.

HOW TO CREATE A WILDLIFE GARDEN

Order of work
- Draw up your designs so that they take into account the house, the boundaries, drains, immovable structures and large trees.
- Dig out and build the pond. A butyl liner is the best option for a natural-looking pond.
- Include an area of bog garden that will take the overflow from the pond.
- Plant the primary trees – these are species that can be found growing wild in your area.
- Underplant the trees with shrubs and ground-cover plants.

Planting
Visit local gardens and see what grows best in your soil. The easiest option is to plant container-grown trees, such as *Betula pendula* (Silver Birch), *Sorbus aucuparia* (Mountain Ash) and *Acers* (Japanese Maples). If you have a small garden, remember to choose compact varieties. Plant the shrubs and ground-cover plants only when the trees are in place. (Note that the seedpods of some species are poisonous.)

Front garden car park

If your front garden is big enough for parking, there is no reason why it cannot be an attractive space. Think carefully about how the car is to be parked in relation to the house and the road, and how the passengers are going to move to and from the car, and then design using smooth curves, attractive paving, plants in brightly coloured containers, small enclosed borders, hanging baskets and climbing plants. Avoid having all-over surfaces like concrete or tarmac.

How can I accommodate my car?

LOOKING AT THE PROJECT

In the design, the front garden is about 4.5 m (15 ft) square, the area to the right of the door is paved with bricks, and there is easy-care planting in the bed.

CONSIDERING THE IMPLICATIONS

If you need to turn the car slightly to get in or out of the space, will this upset the neighbours? Will the lights shine into their windows? Will the car doors bang into their fence? Will you be driving over sewer covers?

VARIATIONS TO CONSIDER

You could have raised beds, so that people cannot easily walk on the plants.

This design cleverly blurs the edge of the paved parking area, and is a good option for a small front garden.

Design guidelines for success

- You need a space no smaller than about 4.5 m (15 ft) square.
- You need good-quality brick paving with a solid foundation.
- Edge the drive with decorative bricks or tiles.
- Include dwarf shrubs and rock-garden plants in the border.
- Mulch around the plants with something like crushed stone or pea gravel.
- Try to blur the edges between the planting and the hardstanding.
- Allow for drainage.

HOW TO CREATE A PARKING GARDEN

Order of work
- Draw up your designs so that they take into account the house, the boundaries, drains, immovable structures and any large trees.
- Mark out the parking area.
- Dig the area out to a depth of 30 cm (1 ft).
- Set a level edge of concrete.
- Put down well-compacted rubble and top it off with bricks bedded in sand – or concrete if the ground is soft.

Planting
Include plants like dwarf conifers and slow-growing alpines – the type of plant that you would grow in a rockery or scree bed (see pages 66–67). Place hanging baskets or containers at the side of the door.

Rock and water garden

From a practical viewpoint, it is a good idea to start with a pond and rocky cascade – the largest you can manage – and then extend it over time to include rock pools and rivulets, a fountain, rocky grottoes, a bog garden, a rockery, a scree bed, side pools, and so on. Working in this way, you will gradually be able to landscape the whole garden, until it is one big rock and water feature. This is a good option if you are short of time or money, or both.

Is this easy to construct?

LOOKING AT THE PROJECT

In the design below, the whole garden has been given over to a mix of rock and water. If it is not water tumbling over rock, then it is a rockery or a scree bed.

CONSIDERING THE IMPLICATIONS

Look carefully at your garden and consider how the design is going to affect the way you use the overall space. Are there going to be problems with children or pets, perhaps?

VARIATIONS TO CONSIDER

You could theme the garden so that it becomes a beach or Japanese garden, or so that it uses a particular type of stone.

This exquisite little garden features just the right mix of cascading water, weathered rock and lush green foliage.

Design guidelines for success

- Decide how much space you want to give over to the project.
- Create the biggest pond that you think you can manage.
- A butyl liner is the best option.
- You need the biggest pump possible.
- Buy local stone in bulk – even if you are not going to use it all for the first stage – because large loads are more cost-effective.
- Work with existing slopes and levels.

HOW TO CREATE A ROCK AND WATER GARDEN

Order of work

- Draw up your designs so that they take into account the house, the boundaries, immovable structures and any large trees.
- Dig out the pond and use the 'spoil' to create a stepped mound that leads into the pond.
- Line the hole and the stepped mound with a sheet of butyl.
- Run a water pipe from the pump in the pond to the top of the mound.
- Build the rock steps and sculpt the remaining area with soil and stone.

Planting

When you come to planting, start at the centre of the pond and work along the edges of the stream, finishing with the rockery and the bog garden. Include items like alpines and dwarf conifers in the rockery, and *Acers* (Japanese Maples) by the waterfall.

Small patio garden

Can I build a small patio?

In much the same way as you can create a wonderfully relaxing, comfortable space in the smallest of rooms, so you can build a small patio. Do not worry in the first instance about style or even materials, but focus on your basic needs. Do you want a small quiet space to read, a place with a table and a couple of comfortable chairs, a place for a barbecue, a place in the sun or shade, or the sound of running water? Let the overall design evolve around your needs.

MAKING THE MOST OF A SMALL SPACE

A dull or ugly area of garden can be dramatically improved by laying a decorative patio design like this one.

A pergola can turn a small patio into an exciting area – it makes the patio feel more defined and solid, as well as private.

A patio can be anything you want it to be. This calm, ordered look draws inspiration from a formal Japanese garden.

LOOKING AT THE PROJECT

Have a good look at your garden. Assess its size in relation to your needs. If you are working in a very small space close to the house, decide how you are going to cover up existing items like drainpipes and disguise manhole covers.

CONSIDERING THE IMPLICATIONS

Just like when you are revamping a room in your house – where you might, for example, draw inspiration from Victorian imagery and then go on to dress the room so that everything corresponds to the original inspiration – you must remember to dress the patio with materials and items that relate to your main idea or theme.

VARIATIONS TO CONSIDER

For patios, there are hundreds of styles, forms and materials to choose from. There are decking patios, brick patios and patios made from bark and gravel. There are patios made from real cut stone and reconstituted stone. There are patios that draw inspiration from all sorts of cultural styles – Mediterranean, Moorish, Japanese, modern. No matter the size of your garden, it is guaranteed that there will be an exciting option just waiting for you.

Although real cut stone pavers are expensive and difficult to fit, they are an exciting option.

Brick and stone look good together, and are perfect if you want to create a low-cost patio.

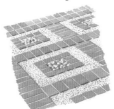

A formal pattern of bricks, with an infill of cobblestones, gravel and plants, is an eye-catching option.

Crazy (cleft stone) paving is a good choice if you want a relatively cheap patio; the stone is bedded on blobs of mortar.

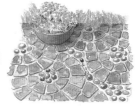

This unusual patio has been embellished with an infill of cobbles pressed into concrete.

Setts come in many types and sizes; salvaged setts from city roads may be obtainable from local authorities.

HOW TO CREATE A SMALL PATIO GARDEN

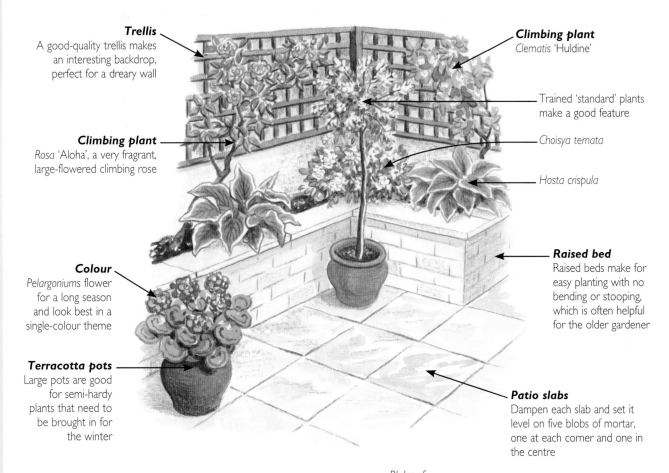

Trellis
A good-quality trellis makes an interesting backdrop, perfect for a dreary wall

Climbing plant
Rosa 'Aloha', a very fragrant, large-flowered climbing rose

Colour
Pelargoniums flower for a long season and look best in a single-colour theme

Terracotta pots
Large pots are good for semi-hardy plants that need to be brought in for the winter

Climbing plant
Clematis 'Huldine'

Trained 'standard' plants make a good feature

Choisya ternata

Hosta crispula

Raised bed
Raised beds make for easy planting with no bending or stooping, which is often helpful for the older gardener

Patio slabs
Dampen each slab and set it level on five blobs of mortar, one at each corner and one in the centre

Modify the project according to your unique situation and preferred materials. This project uses a layer of hardcore (rubble) to stabilize the ground; if you are building on, for example, an existing concrete base, just miss out the hardcore (rubble).

Order of work
Mark out the patio area and clear the topsoil down to a depth of 20 cm (8 in). Dig a 30 cm (1 ft) deep trench for the low wall. Put 10 cm (4 in) of compacted hardcore (rubble) in the trench, followed by 20 cm (8 in) of concrete. Spread 10 cm (4 in) of compacted hardcore (rubble) over the patio area followed by 5 cm (2 in) of sharp sand. Set and level the slabs on blobs of mortar. Build the wall up to about six courses. Paint the walls and fix the trellis.

Planting
Go for plants like hardy fuchsias and *Pelargoniums* in the pots, a mix of climbing roses and *Clematis* up the trellis, and small shrubs of your choice in the raised border. Plant the container-grown shrubs as soon as possible, and the other less hardy plants in due season. Water them in, and carefully monitor their progress.

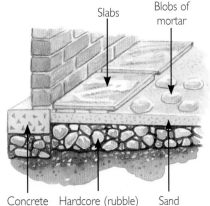

Slabs   Blobs of mortar

Concrete   Hardcore (rubble)   Sand

A cross-section through the project, showing how the various components relate to each other to create a stable, long-lasting patio.

CARE AND MAINTENANCE
Care and maintenance needs to be ongoing. You must remove weeds and moss, prune back vigorous plants, replace any broken pavers, fill gaps with sand mixed with dry concrete by sweeping it into the gaps when wetting it, sweep up the debris, and occasionally scrub with bleach or spray with a high-pressure jet.

Development
Just as you might add to a room inside your house, so you can add to your patio. If, when you are sitting there, you have a fancy for more comfortable chairs, a heater, subtle lights or anything else, then why not just go for it?

Choosing plants

A common problem with beginners to garden design is that, while they have a clear understanding of what they want in the way of structures – paths, patios, ponds, raised borders and so on – they know very little about plants. They then make matters worse by trying to cram their heads full of planting facts. Initially, it is best to focus all your energies on design, and tackle the planting on a need-to-know basis. Keep asking questions – until you know the answers.

WHAT DO YOU NEED TO KNOW?

At this stage, just concentrate on basic facts – things like what such and such a plant needs in the way of soil, shelter, shade and sunlight, how it will look at various times of the year, how big it will grow, and how long it will last. You will eventually want to know about pruning, propagation, diseases and so on, but you can find that out along the way. If you are a complete beginner, make a selection from the following pages of favourite or familiar plants, and then take it from there. Learning by reading is good, but learning by doing is usually much better.

Trees and shrubs

Trees and shrubs are perfect for growing in all gardens; some grow low and broad while others grow very tall. Some are famed for their flowers while others have attractive leaves and berries in autumn and even winter.

Hedges and wall shrubs

Hedges and wall shrubs are just the thing for creating boundaries and for camouflaging an ugly shed or wall. Many wall shrubs benefit from the warmth and protection provided by a wall.

Climbing plants

There are climbing plants for every situation: from ones that cover everything with attractive leaves to those that produce distinctive flowers. Self-climbing and self-supporting climbers are a good option.

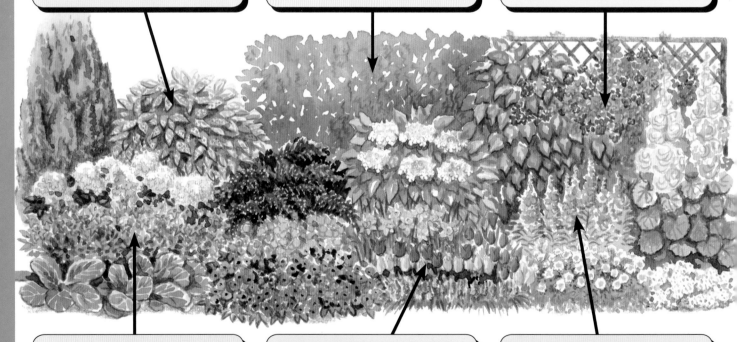

Herbaceous perennials

Herbaceous perennials usually live for 3–4 years before they need to be lifted and divided – perfect for flower borders. In the spring they send up new shoots, which die down to ground level again in the autumn.

Bedding plants and bulbs

Most spring-flowering bedding plants are biennial – they have a two-year life cycle – and look good when grown alongside bulbous plants. Bulbs have an underground storage organ that sees them through dormant periods.

Annuals and biennials

Annuals are raised from seed and grow to flower in the period of one year, while biennials are raised from seed one year and grown to flower the next. Some self-seeding annuals will reappear every year.

Rock, scree and desert plants

There is a huge range of plants that thrive in rocky, scree and desert situations – everything from alpines and dwarf trees through to hardy cacti and succulents.

Water plants

From the side of the pond to the centre, there are bog plants, marginals, deep-water aquatics, and plants that spend their life either floating on the surface or submerged beneath it.

Bamboos and grasses

Bamboos and grasses belong to the same plant family. There are bamboos and grasses for every situation – from small ones that can be grown in pots through to ones that can fill a border.

Container plants

Container plants are simply any plants that are small enough to be grown in containers. While pots can be grouped on the ground, hanging baskets are good for small areas where there is a shortage of floor space.

Herbs

While there is a huge range of herbs to choose from – ones to eat, ones to take as medicine, and ones that smell nice – it is best to grow ones that you can safely eat, meaning the culinary ones that can be used in the kitchen.

Fruit and vegetables

We all know about fruit and vegetables. What better way to enjoy a garden than to watch the plants growing and then to eat the produce?

WHICH PLANTS SUIT MY GARDEN?

The best way of getting an answer to this question is to assess the size of your garden – it might be anything from minute through to small, big, very big or positively huge – and then arm yourself with a pencil and notepad and visit the nearest show garden, followed by a whole range of local gardens, taking note of plants that are thriving.

HOW MANY PLANTS WILL I NEED?

Bearing in mind that plants not only grow in size but can also be increased by seed, cuttings, division and so on, there are two options. You can start off with a few architectural plants like trees, bushes and climbers, and then beg and buy the rest, or you can spend a lot of money instantly filling the garden to overflowing, knowing that very soon you will have to thin the plants out and give them away to friends and family.

BUYING PLANTS

Plants are best purchased from specialists. If you want apple trees, go to a nursery that specializes in apple trees, and so on. In this way, you will get the best product and the best advice. It is always a good idea to arm yourself with a list of questions to ask, so that you end up getting just the right plants.

Garden centres Garden centres are good for small 'one-offs', but they are not good for initial stocking. You should always avoid anything that looks tired and neglected, however.

Nurseries A good nursery is the best option. Try to get your plants from long-established specialists. Call around for the best prices.

Mail order Mail order is fine for the occasional 'one-off', or for some sort of special offer, but that is about it. Certainly be tempted by the pretty photographs, but make sure that you thoroughly research your purchases.

WHAT CAN I GROW FROM SEEDS?

If you are patient and likely to live to a ripe old age, you can grow just about everything from seeds, but they are normally used for annuals, lawns and a whole range of vegetable and salad crops. For some, growing plants from seeds can be a rewarding challenge.

CHOOSING HEALTHY CONTAINER PLANTS

If a plant looks tired, scraggy, dusty, too dry or too wet, or in any way uncared for, it is likely to be a bad buy. Ideally, the plant needs to look compact and clean-stemmed, with no dead or dying bits and no roots growing up from the pot. Don't be tempted by low cost.

IMMEDIATE PLANT CARE

Remove all the straggly bits. Wait for a mild day (not too hot, and not frosty), and then set the plant in position in the garden and give it a generous watering.

Designing with plants

What does this involve?

If you liken the garden with its related structures to a room in your house, the plants are like the wallpaper. The only difference is that the plants are constantly changing in size, shape and colour. Your task, therefore, is not only to select plants that you know will suit the various microclimates that you have around the garden, but also to have some idea of how the ever-changing plants are going to fill the space. Be aware that some plants will rapidly double in size.

POINTS TO CONSIDER

As you work around the garden choosing plants to fill the various spaces, you must make decisions about every plant's suitability. A good way to do this is to ask yourself the following questions.

Sun and shade Is there enough sun or shade? If conditions are not quite right, can you make small modifications by building walls or screens? It might be a sunny position, but are there trees, buildings and the like that will create shade?

Sheltered and exposed Is the plant going to be able to withstand the worst that is going to be thrown at it in the way of wind, rain and frost?

Soil type Is the soil going to suit the plant? If your soil is sandy, does the plant like sandy soil?

Size Is the plant big enough? If it takes time to reach its potential, are you patient enough to wait? If it will eventually be big enough, can you use other plants to fill in the gaps, and then take them out at a later stage?

Personal taste If you like tall and thin, or evergreen, or shrubs that flower for long periods, or whatever it might be, is your plant going to suit?

Cost The initial plant might be expensive, but is this expense going to be offset by the plant's characteristics – the fact that it grows to a huge size or lives a long time, for example?

Maintenance You might like the notion of the plant, but is it going to need a lot of maintenance?

Longevity Is the plant going to live long enough, or even too long, to suit your needs?

Colour Is the plant going to give you plenty of colour? For example, some hardy fuchsias have not only bright flowers and beautiful green foliage but also red berries and red stems.

Contrast and harmony You have chosen two plants – are they going to look good together? Is there enough contrast, or are you looking for plants that are in harmony with each other?

SUITABILITY

Each plant you choose needs to be fitting for its purpose. If you want a plant for, say, a shady, slightly damp space behind a tall wall, then you need to ask yourself two basic questions. Is the plant going to thrive in that position, and, when it reaches maturity, is it going to live up to your design expectations? That is, will it be tall enough, wide enough, the right colour, flower at the right time, be happy alongside your other chosen plants, and so on?

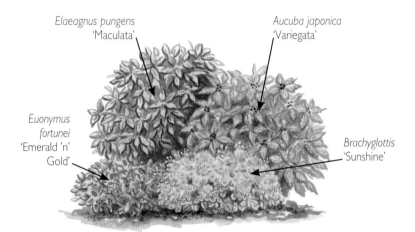

Elaeagnus pungens 'Maculata'

Aucuba japonica 'Variegata'

Euonymus fortunei 'Emerald 'n' Gold'

Brachyglottis 'Sunshine'

This group of shrubs will create colour throughout the year. You could also underplant them with bulbs to enhance the effect even further.

HABIT

A plant's habit has to do with its appearance. Some plants want to grow straight up like a rocket; others want to creep along the ground. The clue to the habit is usually given in the name. For example, a 'prostrate' plant is one that likes to stay very close to the ground, while a 'fastigiate' plant (think of 'fast up') is one that wants to grow upwards.

Combinations of contrasting growth habits can look stunning.

PRACTICALITIES

A plant cannot be *almost right* – it has got to be right in every respect. Sometimes there are so many impracticalities that get in the way – cost, size, sensitivity, unwanted prickles, poisonous berries, unpleasant smell, wrong height, and other disadvantages – that you just have to bite the bullet and choose something else.

EXAMPLES OF PLANTING SCHEMES

A 'mixed' border

Rhododendrons have both eye-catching flowers and beautiful waxy leaves

Evergreens provide form all year round

Acer for brilliant colour

This glorious summer border is made up of shrubs, climbers, small trees, herbaceous perennials, bulbs and bedding plants. A mixed border of this character is especially useful because it will display colour and form throughout the year.

Bamboos and grasses

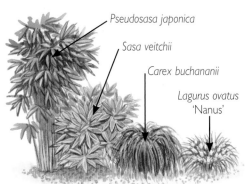

Pseudosasa japonica

Sasa veitchii

Carex buchananii

Lagurus ovatus 'Nanus'

Bamboos and grasses are much favoured for their form and their colour, which changes with the seasons, and they also give useful protection to other plants.

Climbers

Jasminum nudiflorum (Winter-flowering Jasmine) and *Cotoneaster horizontalis*

Tropaeolum speciosum and *Hedera helix* 'Goldheart'

A well-chosen group of climbers gives exciting year-round form and colour. The group on the right consists of Actinidia kolomikta, Eccremocarpus scaber *and* Lonicera japonica *'Halliana'.*

Bedding plants

Impatiens   *Calendula*   *Begonia*   *Petunia*

Bedding plants give a blaze of colour. They can be swiftly changed to suit your requirements, and are a very good standby if other things fall by the wayside, leaving unsightly gaps in the border.

SCENT

Whoever it was that said 'No scents, nonsense, strong scents, good sense' must have enjoyed growing scented plants. Although such plants do not affect the visual design of a garden in the same way as a plant that is strongly shaped and coloured, it is an important consideration, especially if anyone with a visual impairment is likely to visit the garden.

Coloured bark and stems

Brilliant foliage is good, and brightly coloured flowers are great, but there is just as much to be said for startling stem or bark colours. In this context, it is a good idea to walk around a show garden in the autumn and winter, to see just what is on offer.

The dazzling white bark of *Betula pendula* (Silver Birch) and the brilliant red-pink stems of plants like hardy fuchsias and striped or peeling *Acers* (Maples) are wonderfully uplifting in winter, when the world can be a foggy blur of white and grey.

Salix (Willow) – there are many types, sizes and varieties of this popular tree with its colourful stems.

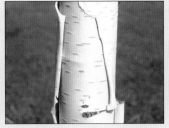

Betula utilis var. jacquemontii has a dazzling white trunk and characteristic peeling bark.

Acer griseum (Paperbark Maple) has dark bark that peels to reveal orange underbark.

Cornus (Dogwood) – commonly called 'Red-stemmed Dogwood' – is favoured for the bright colour of its young stems.

Trees and shrubs

Trees and shrubs are invariably costly, but they are some of the easiest plants to look after, and once they have established themselves in the garden many of them will give you a lifetime of pleasure. It has been said that trees and shrubs form the backbone or framework of the garden. If you take care to choose a good range of trees and shrubs, including winter-, spring- and summer-flowering ones, then you will be able to enjoy year-round colour.

A LITTLE GOES A LONG WAY

If you have a huge garden, you will not need to worry about the size of the trees and shrubs, but otherwise you need to go for small, tight-and-tidy plants – meaning ones that are attractive in themselves. If the character of a tree or shrub is such that you have to keep pruning to keep it in shape, then it is one to be avoided. For the most part, you need items that are slow-growing, attractive throughout the year, easy to establish and non-invasive.

Though many shrubs will live for ten years or more, and of course many trees live for the equivalent of several human lifetimes, they require careful attention – when choosing, during planting, and when pruning. They create a permanent framework for the garden that sets the tone for everything else that goes to create the overall garden style.

Specimen trees and shrubs

A specimen tree or shrub is best thought of as a design feature, like a carefully chosen piece of sculpture. For example, a pair of dwarf evergreens planted in pots, trimmed to shape and placed either side of a flight of steps somehow makes the steps more imposing and grand.

Acer griseum (Paperbark Maple) in all its autumn glory

Amelanchier lamarckii

June Berry UK/USA

Snowy Mespilus UK

Small, deciduous, hardy tree or shrub, with clusters of white flowers in mid-spring. In autumn, the leaves range from deep copper-red through to a gentle yellow, and the red berries turn black.

Soil and situation: likes a moist but well-drained, lime-free soil, in full sun through to dappled shade.

Design notes: a good option for a large garden, against a wall or near a hedge, where you particularly want a small tree or a large, bushy shrub.

↕ 3–4.5 m (10–15 ft) ↔ 3–3.5 m (10–12 ft)

Betula utilis var. jacquemontii

European Silver Birch USA

Silver Birch UK

Himalayan Silver Birch UK

Large, slender tree with green-grey leaves and peeling silver-white bark.

Soil and situation: likes any well-drained soil in situations that range from full sun through to full shade.

Design notes: a good option for a large garden, it looks stunning in a winter landscape.

↕ 6–9 m (20–35 ft) ↔ 1.8–3 m (6–10 ft)

Brachyglottis 'Sunshine'

Syn. *Senecio* 'Sunshine'

Evergreen shrub with silver-grey leaves. The bright yellow, daisy-like flowers are borne in early to mid-summer. The mature bush sits close to the ground like a mossy hump or mound.

Soil and situation: likes a moist, but well-drained, deeply dug soil, in full sun.

Design notes: a good option when you want to draw the eye down to the ground, perhaps around the fringes of a border, or when you want to create an undulating effect.

↕ 60 cm–1.2 m (2–4 ft) ↔ 90 cm–1.5 m (3–5 ft)

Choisya ternata

Mexican Orange Blossom UK/USA

Bushy, evergreen shrub with white orange-blossom-like flowers produced from late spring through to mid-summer. The shrub stands about head height.

Soil and situation: likes a deeply dug, well-drained soil in situations that range from full sun through to dappled shade.

Design notes: a beautiful option when you want a nicely rounded, sweet-smelling, easy-care shrub. Looks good either against a wall or free-standing.

↕ 1.5–1.8 m (5–6 ft) ↔ 1.5–2.1 m (5–7 ft)

Cistus x dansereaui

Rock Rose UK/USA

Sun Rose UK

Bushy, evergreen shrub with papery, red-splashed, white flowers. The rose-like (some say poppy-like) flowers appear from early to mid-summer.

Soil and situation: likes a deeply dug, well-drained soil in full sun; does not like frost or wind.

Design notes: a good traditional choice when you are looking for a large, showy shrub with lots of flowers. Looks good as a pot shrub or in a border.

↕ 30–60 cm (1–2 ft) ↔ 30–60 cm (1–2 ft)

Forsythia x intermedia

Golden Bells UK/USA

Hardy, deciduous shrub with masses of yellow flowers that show from early to mid-spring. The plant glows with golden colour. The mature shrub stands at and above head height.

Soil and situation: likes a deeply dug, moist, well-drained soil in situations from full sun through to dappled shade.

Design notes: a much-loved plant and a good choice for an old-fashioned cottage garden. Good against walls; it can be trimmed to a hedge, but gets straggly if neglected.

↕ 1.8–2.4 m (6–8 ft) ↔ 1.5–2.1 m (5–7 ft)

Fuchsia 'Alice Hoffman'

Bushy, deciduous shrub with red stems, and red and white bell-like flowers from mid-summer to late autumn. There are many other varieties to choose from.

Soil and situation: likes a deeply dug, well-drained soil in situations that range from full sun through to dappled shade.

Design notes: a beautiful traditional option. While this variety can be grown as a feature shrub or cut as a hedge, there are types for every situation – hanging baskets, standing trees in pots and so on. A matched pair of standard fuchsias makes an imposing display.

↕ 1.8–2.4 m (6–8 ft) ↔ 1.5–1.8 m (5–6 ft)

OTHER TREES AND SHRUBS

- *Berberis darwinii* (**Darwin's Berberis**): evergreen shrub with small, spiny leaves, yellow flowers and purple berries. Flowers mid- to late spring. A good choice for hedging when you want a decorative hedge that doubles up as a barrier. Cats, dogs, children and intruders tend to avoid *Berberis*.
- *Buddleja davidii* (**Butterfly Bush/Orange-Eye Buddleia/Summer Lilac**): hardy, deciduous shrub with long, slender stems with spear- or torch-like, purple flowers – looks a bit like a lilac. Flowers mid- to late summer. A very good option for a cottage garden or a wild garden as its beautiful scent attracts butterflies, bees and birds.
- *Cupressus sempervirens* '**Totem Pole**' (**Italian Cypress**): hardy, evergreen tree with small, spear-like leaves. The slender shape speaks of France and the Mediterranean. A good sculptural tree that needs to be 'underwired' (with twine wound around branches, concealed under the leaves) so the shape does not fall apart in the winter.
- *Hydrangea macrophylla* (**Common Hydrangea/French Hydrangea**): hardy, deciduous shrub with ball-like clusters of blue to purple flowers. The flowers appear in mid- to late summer. A 'grow-anywhere' plant, a good choice for beginners. The flowers even look good when they have lost their colour and dried out to papery balls.
- *Prunus* '**Amanogawa**' (**Upright Japanese Cherry**): hardy, lollipop-shaped tree with upright branches carrying clusters of pale pink cherry blossom. A good option when you want a cherry tree but only have a small garden.
- *Taxus baccata* '**Fastigiata Aureomarginata**' (**Gold Yew/Golden Irish Yew**): hardy, evergreen tree with a tall, slender, upright habit, gold-edged leaves and yellow stems. Looks good as a specimen tree – perhaps one set at either side of a gateway or path. Yews have a formal appearance, and they can be trimmed into a neat, crisp outline shape if desired.

Hedges and wall shrubs

How can these be used?

No matter the shape of your garden, you probably have a boundary onto the road, and other boundaries that separate you from your neighbours. You could have wall shrubs disguising an ugly wall, a high, dense hedge on the windward side of the garden, a wide, spiky mix of a hedge and shrubs on one neighbour's side, a stout hedge between you and the school playing fields, and so on. Hedges are good, but be aware that they need constant attention.

HEDGES AND WALL SHRUBS AS BOUNDARIES AND DESIGN FEATURES

Hedges and wall shrubs make the most attractive and long-lasting boundaries. They can be expensive and time-consuming to establish, but once in place they last a lifetime. While time is a killer for walls and wooden fence panels – they crack and crumble as the years go by – hedges and wall shrubs just get stronger and altogether more attractive. Hedges and wall shrubs can be used to add form and colour to the garden. Hedges can be trimmed into just about whatever shape takes your fancy. You can have geometrical forms like cubes and cones, fun forms like animals, or even folly items like arches and seat surrounds. Wall shrubs are perfect for blocking out those ugly walls and grim sheds that some of us just have to live with.

Architectural arch topiary

Topiary arches are winners on three counts – they are eye-catching, they can be used as a divisions or boundaries, and they are great fun to create. If you want to go one step further, you can trim 'windows' on either side of the arch, have castellation, or have secondary arches or niches.

A dramatic arch created from slow-growing Taxus baccata (Yew)

Buxus sempervirens

Common Box USA/UK

Hardy, evergreen shrub with small, dark green leaves. Slow-growing and compact.

Soil and situation: likes well-drained, fertile soil in just about any situation.

Design notes: this is a good plant for small and topiary hedges around herb gardens – just about anywhere where you want to grow a small, tight, traditional, crisp-cut hedge.

⬆ 1.8–2.1 m (6–7 ft) ↔ 1.8–2.1 m (6–7 ft)

Ceanothus thyrsiflorus var. repens

Blue Blossom USA

Californian Lilac UK

Dense, compact, evergreen shrub with small leaves and clusters of brilliant blue flowers in late spring to mid-summer.

Soil and situation: likes well-drained, neutral to acid soil in full sun.

Design notes: a great 'statement' plant, when you really want to create a big smack of eye-catching colour. The blue colour is unusual and long-lasting, and looks wonderful against weathered wood and red bricks.

⬆ 1.2–1.5 m (4–5 ft) ↔ 1.2–1.8 m (4–6 ft)

Cotoneaster horizontalis

Fishbone Cotoneaster USA

Rock Cotoneaster UK

Hardy, low-growing, deciduous shrub with a spreading fan of dense branches. It has small leaves, clusters of pink flowers in spring and brilliant red-orange berries in autumn to late winter.

Soil and situation: likes well-drained soil in situations that range from full sun through to dappled shade.

Design notes: a good option when you want to cover a dull wall or fence with a splash of colour, particularly in winter when the berries are showing.

⬆ 60–90 cm (2–3 ft) ↔ 1.2–1.8 m (4–6 ft)

Euonymus radicans 'Silver Queen'

Common Radicans UK

Japonica USA

Dense, low-growing, evergreen shrub with small, variegated leaves. The flowers appear in late spring to mid-summer.

Soil and situation: likes well-drained, neutral to acid soil in full sun.

Design notes: good as a wall shrub or low hedge, and much favoured in coastal areas. Looks good growing against white-rendered block walls.

↕ 60–90 cm (2–3 ft)　↔ 60–90 cm (2–3 ft)

Fuchsia magellanica 'Riccartonii'

Fuchsia USA/UK

Dense, compact, deciduous shrub with dark green leaves, red stems, and clusters of brilliant crimson and purple, bell-like flowers from mid-summer through to autumn.

Soil and situation: likes well-drained soil in full sun through to dappled shade – does best in a frost-free area.

Design notes: an easy-care, good-value shrub with beautiful flowers and just as beautiful red stems. You can have it as a wall shrub, or trimmed to make a hedge.

↕ 1.2–1.5 m (4–5 ft)　↔ 1.2–1.8 m (4–6 ft)

Lavandula stoechas

French Lavender USA/UK

Spanish Lavender USA/UK

Tender, evergreen shrub with grey-green leaves and tufts of pink flowers.

Soil and situation: likes well-drained, fertile soil in full sun or dappled shade.

Design notes: this plant has long been used as low, aromatic hedging. Looks good as a low hedge around herb gardens, around patios – anywhere where you want to sit and enjoy the soothing aroma.

↕ 30–60 cm (1–2 ft)　↔ 30–60 cm (1–2 ft)

Santolina chamaecyparissus

Cotton Lavender USA/UK

Lavender Cotton USA/UK

Hardy, bushy, dense, dome-like, evergreen shrub with silver leaves and bright yellow flowers in mid- to late summer.

Soil and situation: likes well-drained, neutral soil in full sun.

Design notes: a plant traditionally used to create decorative, low, aromatic hedges. Would be good around a sitting area such as a bower or patio.

↕ 60–90 cm (2–3 ft)　↔ 30–60 cm (1–2 ft)

OTHER WALL SHRUBS AND HEDGE PLANTS

- *Abutilon megapotamicum:* semi-hardy wall shrub with a generous show of red-purple flowers from summer to autumn. A good choice when you want a long season of colour. Height: 1.5–2.1 m (5–7 ft). Spread: 1.5–2.1 m (5–7 ft).

- x *Cupressocyparis leylandii* 'Robinson's Gold' (Leyland Cypress): a swift-growing conifer with bronze-yellow foliage. Although this plant has slightly fallen out of favour, it is still a good option for large gardens, when there is a need for a dense hedge. If you cut it back three times in the growing season you will be able, for a moment or two, to fool the eye into believing it is a yew hedge. Height: 1.8–4.5 m (6–15 ft). Spread: 0.9–1.2 m (3–4 ft).

- *Fagus sylvatica* (Beech): hardy, deciduous plant, with green leaves turning to russet in autumn. The russet leaves stay in place for most of the winter. A strong beech hedge is a traditional feature, good for town and country gardens alike. A 9 m (30 ft) high beech hedge can be quite an impressive sight. Height: 1.2–9 m (4–30 ft). Spread: 0.9–1.5 m (3–5 ft).

- *Ilex aquifolium* (Holly): hardy, evergreen plant with spiky leaves – the male form has bright red berries. This is the hedge to choose if you are trying to create an impenetrable barrier. Cats, dogs and children will stay away from the fallen leaves that gradually form an undercarpet around it. Height: 0.9–7.5 m (3–25 ft). Spread: 0.6–1.2 m (2–4 ft).

- *Piptanthus nepalensis* (Evergreen Laburnum): nearly an evergreen, it produces large, bright yellow flowers. It needs the protection of a warm, wind-sheltered wall. Height: 0.9–1.5 m (3–5 ft). Spread: 0.9–2.4 m (3–8 ft).

- *Prunus spinosa* (Sloe/Blackthorn): hardy, deciduous plant with white flowers and purple sloe berries that makes an impenetrable hedge. This is a good option for a country garden that backs onto a field with sheep or cattle. Height: 0.9–1.5 m (3–5 ft). Spread: 0.9–2.4 m (3–8 ft).

Climbing plants

How can I best use climbers?

Climbing plants have evolved in such a way that they are able to climb up or around a vertical or horizontal support. Some twist and twine around wires, rods and host plants, some send out aerial roots so that they can climb up brick and stonework, some have tendrils for clinging onto trellis and host plants, and some have a vigorous, bunching growth that enables them to scramble up a support. If you are looking for swift, high plants, climbers are the answer.

CLIMBING PLANTS AS DESIGN FEATURES

You have covered the ground with shrubs, bushes, trees, grass and so on, and you have put hedges around the boundaries of the garden, so now what can you do? The answer is to create what has been called the 'vertical' part of the garden, and there are climbing plants for just about every situation that you can imagine. You could have them climbing over ugly items that are beyond your control, such as unsightly sheds and crumbling walls, you could use them to provide shade or to create private rooms within your garden, you could drape them over structures such as pergolas and arches, you could grow them on supports in containers, you could let them scramble through and over trees – there are countless options.

Front-door flowers

What can you do about a dismal front door? The answer is to build a wooden porch, put up trellis and have climbing plants all around. One moment you have something like the front door to 'Bleak House' and the next you have a friendly and inviting grand entrance with lots of glorious form, foliage and colour.

Climbers and containers make a riot of colour.

Clematis 'Etoile Violette'

Deciduous climber with dark green leaves and amazing mauve flowers from late spring to mid-summer.

Soil and situation: likes well-drained soil in full sun, as long as the roots are well covered.

Design notes: a great plant to have climbing up and over a trellis or a bower seat – a plant prized for its flowers.

⬆ 1.8–3 m (6–10 ft) ↔ 1.2–1.8 m (4–6 ft)

Clematis flammula

Fragrant Virgin's Bower UK/USA

Vigorous climber with dark green leaves, purple stems and clusters of star-like, yellow-cream flowers from mid-summer to mid-autumn.

Soil and situation: likes rich, well-drained soil in full sun.

Design notes: the perfect climber for growing over a summerhouse or pergola – the scent is wonderful on a warm summer's afternoon.

⬆ 6 m (20 ft) ↔ 1.2–1.8 m (4–6 ft)

Clematis hybrids

Deciduous climbers with striking flowers. Depending upon the variety, they flower from early to late summer, with hues ranging from solid colour through to blooms that are variously splashed and striped with colour.

Soil and situation: likes well-drained, neutral to alkaline soil in full sun, with the roots in shade.

Design notes: *Clematis* are the show-offs of the climbing world. If you really want to go to town with a climbing plant, then *Clematis* hybrids are a good option. They look good climbing over fences and trellis.

⬆ 1.2–4.5 m (4–15 ft) ↔ 1.2–3 m (4–10 ft)

Fallopia baldschuanica syn. Polygonum baldschuanicum

Mile-a-minute Vine UK/USA

Russian Vine UK/USA

Rampant climber with pale green leaves and fluffy, creamy pink flowers from mid-summer to mid-autumn.

Soil and situation: likes well-drained soil in situations ranging from full sun through to dappled shade.

Design notes: if you want to cover an unsightly building or boundary quickly, this is the ultimate answer.

↑ 12 m (40 ft) ↔ 12–18 m (40–60 ft)

Ipomoea tricolor

Morning Glory UK/USA

Semi-hardy annual with a light leaf cover, and blue, red or mauve, bell-shaped flowers from late summer to early autumn. At a quick glance, it looks a bit like a runner-bean plant.

Soil and situation: likes most soils in full sun.

Design notes: a good old-time favourite for traditional cottage gardens. Looks best draped over sheds and other structures.

↑ 2.4–3 m (8–10 ft) ↔ 2.4–3 m (8–10 ft)

Lathyrus odoratus

Sweet Pea UK/USA

Delicate climbing plant (there are lots of varieties) with beautiful, often fragrant, butterfly-like flowers from mid-summer to mid-spring.

Soil and situation: likes well-drained soil in full sun.

Design notes: Sweet Peas look so delicate and yet are hardy – the perfect answer for beginners to gardening. If you are planning a cottage garden, or looking to embellish a wall in a town garden, Sweet Peas are an attractive option.

↑ 1.8–2.4 m (6–8 ft) ↔ 1.8–2.4 m (6–8 ft)

Passiflora caerulea

Blue Passionflower UK/USA

Deciduous climber with stunningly beautiful flowers from summer to autumn, followed by bright orange, egg-sized fruits.

Soil and situation: likes well-drained soil in full sun.

Design notes: a fascinating plant – the fruits are just like big orange eggs. The flowers only open on sunny days when they are looking towards the sun.

↑ 3–9 m (10–30 ft) ↔ 1.5–9 m (5–30 ft)

Trachelospermum jasminoides

Star Jasmine UK/USA

Vigorous, hardy climber with dark green leaves and delicate, white, star-shaped flowers from mid- to late summer.

Soil and situation: likes well-drained soil in full sun but it can tolerate dappled sunlight.

Design notes: with the flowers being modest but fragrant, this climber is grown more for its foliage. Good plant for a bower or pergola.

↑ 1.2–1.5 m (4–5 ft) ↔ 1.2–1.8 m (4–6 ft)

OTHER CLIMBING PLANTS

- *Campsis* x *tagliabuana* (**Trumpet Creeper**): vigorous climber with trumpet-shaped, orange-red flowers. Once established it flowers from summer to autumn.
- *Lonicera* (**Honeysuckle/Wild Woodbine**): climber with masses of leaves and creamy yellow flowers. Looks best when it is left alone, especially in a country garden.
- *Parthenocissus tricuspidata* 'Veitchii' (**Boston Ivy**): densely foliaged shrub that turns dark to crimson-purple in the autumn. If you want to block out an ugly wall, this is a good option.
- *Tropaeolum majus* (**Climbing Nasturtium**): annual with green leaves and poppy-like, orange flowers, just like the ordinary Nasturtium. Ideal for quick colour.
- *Wisteria sinensis* (**Chinese Wisteria**): vigorous climber with hanging bunches of brilliant blue-purple flowers. This plant does take a long time to establish, but once it has done so will last a lifetime.

Herbaceous perennials

Herbaceous perennials are all the green, 'non-woody' plants that just pop up year after year. They have a long-lived rootstock, and stems and leaves that die down annually. Perennials burst into fresh green growth in the spring, flower in late spring or summer, or early autumn, and generally multiply throughout the year, all before dying back in the autumn. They are almost indestructible, usually pest-free plants, and represent a good-value, relatively easy option.

What does 'herbaceous' mean?

HERBACEOUS PERENNIALS AS DESIGN FEATURES

Traditionally, herbaceous perennials have been grown in borders with walls and fences as a backdrop – and of course they do fine in this position – but there is no reason why they should not be planted in island beds, in containers, on the fringes of wooded areas, or wherever takes your fancy. The wonderful thing is that you can let them do their thing year after year, without doing much more than cutting them back at the end of the season. After about four years, dig them up, throw away the woody centre, hack the remaining ring into sections, and then plant these out and start again. From a design viewpoint, the trick is knowing about size and colour. Look at display gardens so that you have some idea as to your chosen plant's potential.

Perennials on patios

Perennials can look great on patios, balconies and roof gardens. All you need to do is choose a selection of small, hardy plants, set them out in good-sized tubs – so that each

tub becomes a showpiece specimen – let them all perform for 2–3 years until they are crowded out, and then lift and divide them, and start the cycle again.

A low-cost, large display option for a patio, deck or roof garden.

Achillea 'Moonshine'

Milfoil Yarrow UK/USA

Hardy plant with fern-like leaves and large clusters of yellow, daisy-like flowers from early to late summer.

Soil and situation: does well in poor soil in full sun.

Design notes: a good choice for rockeries and dry scree gardens. The flowers and foliage look particularly good when the plants are mulched with something like grey-coloured grit or washed crushed shells.

 30 cm (1 ft) ↔ 30 cm (1 ft)

Alstroemeria 'Golden Crest'

Peruvian Lily UK/USA

Delicate-looking, slightly tender perennial with clusters of brilliantly exotic, tiger-striped, orange, lily-like flowers in mid-summer.

Soil and situation: likes well-drained but moist soil in situations from full sun to dappled shade; avoid exposed sites.

Design notes: looks its best planted in swathes when you want to create a lush, rich effect. Would also look good as a feature in a patio garden, so that it can be viewed close up.

60–90 cm (2–3 ft) ↔ 30–60 cm (1–2 ft)

Hosta 'Wide Brim'

Funkia UK

Plantain Lily UK/USA

Hosta USA

Hardy plant from Japan with yellow-green leaves and small, white flowers; it is grown mainly for its foliage.

Soil and situation: likes well-drained, moist soil in dappled and full shade.

Design notes: looks its best in shady borders that fringe the edges of woodland, and is perfect for a Japanese garden. The disadvantage is that slugs also find it very attractive and may create holes in the leaves.

30–60 cm (1–2 ft) ↔ 60–90 cm (2–3 ft)

Iris ensata 'Yoake Mae'

Hardy, tall iris with deep, rich, mauve-purple flowers in late spring and bold, green leaves – very lush. There are many other varieties.

Soil and situation: likes well-drained, moist soil in dappled sunlight.

Design notes: irises are choice plants for damp borders and around ponds – meaning soil that is wet without being waterlogged. Some irises thrive with their roots in water, however. Although the flowers tend to be short-lived, they are spectacular.

↕ 60–90 cm (2–3 ft) ↔ 30–60 cm (1–2 ft)

Monarda didyma 'Cambridge Scarlet'

Bee Balm UK/USA

Hardy perennial with light green leaves and spiky scarlet flowers borne in mid- to late summer.

Soil and situation: likes well-drained but moist soil in situations ranging from full sun through to dappled shade.

Design notes: a good-looking plant with leaves that are aromatic when crushed. This is a good plant for patio borders and for around seating areas. It could be included in a scented garden.

↕ 30–60 cm (1–2 ft) ↔ 30–60 cm (1–2 ft)

Paeonia

Peony UK/USA

Hardy, leafy plants with strikingly beautiful, single and double flowers that range in colour from white to salmon-pink, crimson and rose-red. Over the whole range of types, they flower from early to mid-summer.

Soil and situation: likes well-drained, moist soil in sheltered situations from full sun through to dappled shade.

Design notes: they look particularly good massed in borders; a classic option for open borders and for woodland fringes. They are much loved in Japan, so they have a place in a Japanese garden.

↕ 30–90 cm (1–3 ft) ↔ 30–60 cm (1–2 ft)

Salvia sclarea var. turkestanica

Clary Sage UK/USA

Hardy perennial with spiky, white and purple flowers in mid-summer.

Soil and situation: likes well-drained but moist soil in situations ranging from full sun to dappled shade.

Design notes: although this plant looks good and performs well year after year, some people find the aroma less than pleasant.

↕ 0.9–1.2 m (3-4 ft) ↔ 60–90 cm (2–3 ft)

OTHER HERBACEOUS PERENNIALS

- *Allium moly* (**Golden Garlic**): hardy plant with strap-shaped leaves and clusters of yellow, star-like flowers. Grows rapidly into solid-looking, football-sized clumps – good for new gardens.
- *Aruncus dioicus* (**Goat's Beard**): hardy plant with lax, terminal heads of creamy-white flowers produced during early summer.
- *Bergenia cordifolia* (**Elephant's Ear**): hardy plant with leathery, green leaves and drooping heads of bell-shaped, pink flowers. A good old-time favourite that grows anywhere and always looks interesting.
- *Convallaria majalis* (**Lily-of-the-valley**): hardy plant with upright, green leaves and delicate, white, bell-shaped flowers. Looks its best in borders under windows, and in swathes around trees and alongside paths. One of those plants that can stand a good amount of neglect.
- *Filipendula ulmaria* (**Meadowsweet**): very popular, hardy plant with masses of dark green leaves and fluffy, white-cream flowers that smell of almonds. A choice plant for the outer fringes of a bog garden or the edge of a woodland area.
- *Hemerocallis citrina* (**Daylily**): hardy plant with strap-like leaves and orange, star-like flowers. Another plant that you can just dig in and leave to get on with it. On a warm evening it gives off a beautiful, sweet, honeysuckle-like scent.
- *Phlox paniculata* (**Summer Phlox/Fall Phlox**): hardy plant with upright stems, green leaves and pinky purple flowers. Looks beautiful when growing in large drifts along the edges of paths, trailed alongside a wooded area, in narrow borders or around a patio.
- *Stachys byzantina* (**Lamb's Ear/Lamb's Tongue**): half-hardy plant with distinctive leaves that are covered with silvery hairs. During mid-summer it bears purple flowers.
- *Trollius x cultorum* (**Globe Flower**): hardy, moisture-loving plant with large, buttercup-like flowers borne during late spring and early summer.

Bedding plants

What does 'bedding' mean?

The 'bedding method' involves autumn planting of plants that will flower in the following spring, and then in late spring removing the whole display and starting again with plants that will flower in the summer. Although bedding plants can be just about anything that fits into this scheme, they are usually broken down into two groups: spring-flowering bulbs, biennials and perennials, and summer-flowering annuals and tender perennials.

BEDDING PLANTS AS DESIGN FEATURES

Traditionally, bedding schemes were incredibly complex, with intricately shaped borders and plants set out in all manner of patterns and colours, but there is now a move to having either very simple geometrical forms, like circles or ovals, or beds that are completely free-form in shape, with the plants being in random drifts rather than formal patterns. As for the plants, you can have bulbs, biennials, perennials, annuals or whatever you like. The trick is to choose the right plant height and spread, so that you finish up with a well-packed bed without any gaps. A good idea is to visit show gardens that specialize in informal beds, and public parks that excel in formal patterns, and to take note of what is going on in terms of colour, shape and type of plant.

Bedding on balconies

Bedding displays can look beautiful on balconies. Just select your plants, much as you would for a small bed, and then plant them out in hanging-baskets, windowboxes and tubs. You could have bright red *Pelargoniums*, *Lysimachia nummularia* 'Aurea' trailing over the edge of the balcony, and so on.

A beautiful, bold balcony display can give much pleasure to passers-by.

Alcea rosea

Hollyhock (UK/USA)

Also known as *Althaea rosea*, this hardy perennial is usually grown as a biennial, and occasionally as an annual. From mid- to late summer it has tall stems with flowers in colours including yellow, pink, red and white. Some have double flowers.

Soil and situation: fertile, moisture-retentive soil in a sheltered position.

Design notes: a useful plant for cloaking an ugly wall or fence panel.

↕ 1.5–1.8 m (5–6 ft) ↔ 45–60 cm (1½–2 ft)

Antirrhinum

Snapdragon UK/USA

Summer-flowering plants with trumpet- or nose-shaped flowers. Children enjoy using the flowers as finger puppets.

Soil and situation: likes well-drained, moist soil; best in a sunny but sheltered position.

Design notes: a good option in that they flower from summer right through to early autumn. There are types for every situation – miniature, intermediate and tall. Good choice for pink-red schemes.

↕ 30–90 cm (1–3 ft) ↔ 30–60 cm (1–2 ft)

Bellis perennis

Common Daisy UK/USA

Hardy biennial with white, carmine, pink or cherry-red flowers from early spring to autumn.

Soil and situation: likes well-drained, moist soil in sheltered situations that range from full sun to dappled shade.

Design notes: the shape of the Common Daisy makes it a good filler when you want a bright, punchy little flower to bridge the gaps.

↕ 5–10 cm (2–4 in) ↔ 7.5–10 cm (3–4 in)

Campanula medium

Canterbury Bell (UK/USA)

Hardy biennial with upright stems bearing white, pink, blue or violet bell-shaped flowers from late spring to mid-summer.

Soil and situation: moderately fertile, well-drained soil in full sun.

Design notes: there are lots to choose from and they are perfect for cottage gardens.

↕ 38–90 cm (15–90 cm) ↔ 23–30 cm (9–12 in)

Impatiens

Hardy or tender annual, depending on the type. The common Balsam type ranges in colour from scarlet, red and salmon-pink to mauve, purple and white. The flowers appear from early to late summer.

Soil and situation: does well in poor, gritty soil in full sun.

Design notes: because the Balsam *Impatiens* was very popular a century or so ago, it is now commonly used to create a dreamy, old-time look, with the flowers being seen as drifts rather than patterns.

↕ 30–60 cm (1–2 ft) ↔ 30 cm (1 ft))

Petunia

Half-hardy annual with tight, trumpet-shaped flowers in a wide range of colours and sizes.

Soil and situation: likes well-drained, moist soil in a sunny, sheltered position.

Design notes: petunias are very showy flowers – perfect for summer bedding. Good choice for a traditional, cottage-type country garden.

↕ 30 cm (1 ft) ↔ 30 cm (1 ft)

Tagetes patula

French Marigold UK/USA

Half-hardy annual with striking, ruffled, ball-shaped, yellow-orange flowers from summer to autumn. There is a wide range of sizes and colours – lots of yellows and oranges.

Soil and situation: likes well-drained, moist, slightly poor soil in sunny situations.

Design notes: there are lots of varieties to choose from, making this a choice bedding plant.

↕ 20–90 cm (8 in–3 ft) ↔ 30–90 cm (1–3 ft)

OTHER BEDDING PLANTS

- *Asarina purpusii* **'Victoria Falls':** half-hardy summer-bedding plant with a gushing mass of purple flowers with long trumpets. Trails to 60 cm (2 ft).
- *Begonia semperflorens* **'Stara Mixed' (Fibrous Begonia/Waxed Begonia):** half-hardy summer-bedding plant with white, rose and scarlet flowers. Height: 30 cm (1 ft). Spread: 30 cm (1 ft).
- *Bidens ferulifolia* **'Golden Eye':** half-hardy summer-bedding plant with yellow, star-like flowers and fern-like foliage. Height: to 30 cm (1 ft). Spread: tumbling.
- *Erysimum alpinum* **(Alpine Wallflower):** hardy spring-bedding plant with masses of yellow and mauve flowers. Height: to 15 cm (6 in). Spread: 15 cm (6 in).
- *Erysimum cheiri* **(Wallflower/English Wallflower):** hardy spring-bedding plant with colours including orange, red and rose pink. Height: to 30 cm (1 ft). Spread: 20 cm (8 in).
- *Lunaria annua* **(Honesty/Silver Dollar):** hardy biennial with fragrant, purple flowers from late spring to early summer, followed by attractive seedpods. Height: to 90 cm (3 ft). Spread: to 30 cm (1 ft).
- *Myosotis sylvatica* **(Forget-me-not):** hardy spring-bedding plant with characteristic, misty-blue flowers. There are lots of shades of blue. Height: to 30 cm (1 ft). Spread: 15 cm (6 in).
- *Primula* x *polyantha* **(Polyanthus):** hardy spring-bedding plants with flowers ranging from crimson, blue and pink to yellow, white and cream. Height and spread: variable.
- *Viola* **'Universal Citrus Mixed' (Garden Pansy):** hardy summer-bedding plant with orange, yellow or white, pansy-like flowers. Height: to 20 cm (8 in). Spread: 25 cm (10 in).
- *Zinnia elegans* **(Youth and Old Age):** half-hardy summer-bedding plant with colours ranging from white and purple to yellow, orange, red and pink. Height: to 90 cm (3 ft). Spread: 60 cm (2 ft).

Annuals and biennials

What is the difference?

Annuals are plants that go through their whole lifecycle in one season, and biennials are plants that do it over a two-year period. Remember, however, that much depends on the specific plant and the climate you are growing it in. For example, a tender plant that will happily grow as a perennial in a warm region might need to be grown as an annual in a colder area. Some annuals are also successful at self-seeding, reappearing in the garden year after year.

ANNUALS AND BIENNIALS AS DESIGN FEATURES

The big question here for beginners to garden design, and one that pops up time after time, is – if annuals mature in one year and biennials in two, is it possible to start out with a bare-plot garden and fill it with colour in the same year? The swift answer is yes, and here is how to do it.

Let us say that you are starting in late summer or early autumn. You can buy in carefully selected pot-grown biennials and plant them out straight away. Then, in the following late spring or early summer, you can sow seeds of half-hardy annuals like Phlox, Asters and Marigolds. In this way, at the end of it all, by late summer – within a 12-month period – you will have had both annuals and biennials in bloom in your previously bare garden.

Portable planting

If you are working in a very small space, such as a verandah, and are really unclear about terms like 'hardy' and 'half-hardy', then plant your annuals and biennials in portable containers – pots, baskets, tubs – and then make decisions about bringing them in and putting them out as you go along.

An eye-catching combination of colour and form can be created.

Anagallis monelli
Blue Pimpernel UK/USA

Half-hardy annual with tight habit, with blue flowers in summer. Sow outside in mid-spring to flower in the summer of the same year.

Soil and situation: likes well-drained, moist soil in a sunny, sheltered position.

Design notes: a beautiful feature of this plant is the fact that the flowers open and close with the sun. This being so, it is important to plant them in open, fully sunny positions.

↕ 15–25 cm (6–10 in) ↔ 15–25 cm (6–10 in)

Datura meteloides 'Evening Fragrance'
Angel's Trumpet UK/USA

Thorn Apple UK/USA

Perennial, usually treated as a half-hardy annual, with large, trumpet-shaped, white and lavender flowers. Sow under glass in spring, and plant out in early summer to flower in mid- and late summer.

Soil and situation: likes well-drained, moist, light soil in sunny situations.

Design notes: good traditional choice for borders, but also looks good as a specimen in a pot or tub. Can produce flowers up to 20 cm (8 in) long.

↕ 0.9–1.2 m (3–4 ft) ↔ 60–90 cm (2–3 ft)

Eschscholzia californica
Californian Poppy (UK/USA)

Hardy annual with blue-green leaves and masses of bright orange-yellow flowers from early to late summer. Colour range now includes scarlet, crimson, rose, orange, yellow, white and red.

Soil and situation: light, poor, well-drained soil in full sun.

Design notes: these flowers are bright and tend to dominate. Ideal for informal schemes.

↕ 30–38 cm (12–15 in) ↔ 15–23 cm (6–9 in)

Myosotis sylvatica

Forget-me-not UK/USA

Hardy biennial with swathes of misty blue flowers. Sow in early spring, and plant in final positions in autumn to flower the following spring.

Soil and situation: likes well-drained, moist soil – best in a sunny but sheltered position.

Design notes: though they look good in borders, especially fringing a woodland, they also do well in rock gardens and containers.

↕ 30 cm (1 ft) ↔ 15 cm (6 in)

Nicotiana 'Avalon Lime and Purple Bicolor'

Tobacco plant UK/USA

Half-hardy annual with a compact habit and large, lime and purple, star-shaped flowers. Sow under glass in late winter to early spring, and plant out the seedlings in late spring.

Soil and situation: likes well-drained, moist soil in sunny beds.

Design notes: although this is a good option for planting in large beds and borders, it also looks good massed in a container. Suits a 'tropical' garden.

↕ 20–30 cm (8–12 in) ↔ 20–30 cm (8–12 in)

Petunia 'Prism Sunshine'

Half-hardy annual with striking, bell- or trumpet-shaped, yellow-green and cream flowers. Sow under glass in late winter and plant out in early summer.

Soil and situation: likes well-drained, moist soil in sunny situations.

Design notes: there are so many varieties that you can have petunias just about everywhere – in beds and containers, in pots in the conservatory, in hanging-baskets and in windowboxes. There are lots of colours and textures to choose from.

↕ 20–30 cm (8–12 in) ↔ 30–60 cm (1–2 ft)

Primula x polyantha

Primrose UK/USA

Hardy biennials with yellow, creamy white, pink or crimson flowers in spring. Sow in late spring or early summer, and plant out in late summer or early autumn to flower the following spring.

Soil and situation: likes well-drained, slightly sandy soil in situations ranging from full sun to dappled shade.

Design notes: there are primulas in just about every shape and size you can imagine. The Common Primrose and the Cowslip take a lot of beating, especially when planted on woodland banks.

↕ 15–25 cm (6–10 in) ↔ 15–25 cm (6–10 in)

OTHER ANNUALS AND BIENNIALS

- *Ageratum houstonianum* (**Floss Flower/Pussy Foot**): half-hardy annual with bluish flowers. There are many varieties in lots of colours.
- *Asarina purpusii* '**Victoria Falls**': half-hardy annual summer-bedding plant with a gushing mass of purple flowers with long trumpets; trails up to 60 cm (2 ft).
- *Chrysanthemum carinatum* (**Annual Chrysanthemum/Tricolored Chrysanthemum**): also known as *Chrysanthemum tricolor*, this hardy annual has large, daisy-like flowers with contrasting colour bandings.
- *Dianthus barbatus* (**Sweet William**): hardy summer-flowering biennial with clusters of delicate, daisy-like flowers in colours that range from pink through to scarlet. Though technically a perennial, it is best treated as a biennial and raised from seed each year.
- *Digitalis* (**Foxglove**): biennial that produces delicate, rose-purple, thimble-shaped flowers. It makes a wonderful border plant and is good for shady positions and edges of woodland.
- *Echium vulgare* (**Viper's Bugloss**): fully hardy biennial with tall spikes of violet-purple flowers. This plant is a good option for a seaside garden, or for a scrubby wild corner.
- *Heliotropium arborescens* (**Cherry Pie/Heliotrope**): half-hardy perennial, invariably grown as a half-hardy annual. Fragrant, forget-me-not-like flowers, in colours ranging from dark violet, through lavender, to white.
- *Lunaria annua* (**Honesty**): hardy biennial with purplish flowers followed by silver seedpods. The dried pods make very attractive winter decorations.
- *Pelargonium* Cascade Series (**Balcon/Continental Geraniums**): half-hardy annual with trailing drifts and mounds of flowers.
- *Verbascum thapsus* (**Aaron's Rod**): fully hardy biennial with bold rosettes of silvery-white leaves topped with a spike of yellow flowers. This plant is often seen growing wild.

Rock, scree and desert plants

Rock, scree and desert are 'shorthand' for geographical scenarios – a rocky mountainside, a scree-covered slope, and a desert. The common factor with rock, scree and desert plants is that they have all, to a greater or lesser degree, adapted themselves in order to thrive in harsh conditions where the soil is not much more than stone, grit and sand, and the weather is an extreme mix of very wet, very dry, very hot and very cold. This makes them useful for 'difficult' spots.

What type of plants are these?

ROCK, SCREE AND DESERT PLANTS AS DESIGN FEATURES

Although each of these types of plant needs different soil and water conditions – swifter drainage, long periods without water and so on – they can all be grown against a backdrop of rock, sand and scree. From a designer's viewpoint, this is exciting in that it provides a chance to get away from traditional gardens that need lots of water, rich soil, bedding plants, and so on – and allows them to try their hand at 'low-maintenance dry gardening'. Some designers also see rock, scree and desert gardens as being a good way, in a world where climates are rapidly changing, to create a uniquely different type of garden. Draw inspiration from places in nature – rocky gulches, gravel pits and such like – where plants grow against all the odds.

Weathered wood

If you want to go one step further and extend the dry rock theme, you could miss out on figurative sculptures and go for a completely naturalistic effect. Weathered wood looks particularly good set against a backdrop of rock, sand and scree.

A dry garden with found sculpture.

Agave americana 'Variegatum'

Century Plant UK/USA

Distinctive succulent that produces very tall flower spikes, 4.5–6 m (15–20 ft) in height. Some types only flower in maturity and then die.

Soil and situation: likes very well-drained, poor, porous soil in a very sunny, dry position.

Design notes: this plant is grown more for its exotic 'desert' looks than anything else – perfect for a dry courtyard, dry patio garden, or dry Mediterranean garden.

↕ 0.9–1.8 m (3–6 ft) ↔ 1.8–2.7 m (6–9 ft)

Artemisia armeniaca

Lad's Love UK/USA

Southernwood UK/USA

Wormwood UK/USA

Hardy shrub with silvery-grey leaves and small, yellow flowers.

Soil and situation: likes very well-drained soil in a sunny, dry position.

Design notes: while this plant needs more water than some of the other 'dry' plants, it does look the part. A good option for a themed garden, when you want a dry, grey look with lots of sand, stone and bleached wood.

↕ 30–90 cm (1–3 ft) ↔ 30–90 cm (1–3 ft)

Aurinia saxatilis syn. *Alyssum saxatile*

Gold Dust UK/USA

Hardy, shrubby evergreen with grey-green leaves and clusters of yellow flowers produced from mid-spring to early summer.

Soil and situation: likes very well-drained soil in a sunny, dry position.

Design notes: this plant goes well with a silver-grey, dry sand or scree theme.

↕ 20–25 cm (8–10) ↔ 30–60 cm (1–2 ft)

Eryngium

Sea Holly UK/USA

Hardy, bushy, thistle-like herbaceous perennials with vivid blue flowerheads, 4.5–6 m (15–20 ft) in length.

Soil and situation: likes very well-drained, poor soil in a very sunny, dry position.

Design notes: looks stunningly beautiful against dry sand or scree. It is grown more for its colour and texture than anything else, and is perfect for a dry courtyard, dry patio garden or a dry Mediterranean garden.

↕ 0.9–1.8 m (3–6 ft) ↔ 1.8–2.7 m (6–9 ft)

Juniperus

Juniper UK/USA

Hardy, evergreen tree or shrub that is compact and slow-growing with small, spiky, scale-like leaves.

Soil and situation: likes well-drained, poor, slightly chalky soil in a sunny, dry position.

Design notes: the slow-growing characteristics of this plant makes it perfect for a dry rock, scree or sandy garden with a desert, Mediterranean, large rockery or high mountain theme. There are lots of varieties – some upright and others dwarf and spreading.

↕ 0.9–1.2 m (3–4 ft) ↔ 30–90 cm (1–3 ft)

Opuntia ficus-indica

Indian Fig UK/USA

Prickly Pear UK/USA

Exotic succulent with luscious yellow, orange or red flowers on the upper part of the joints. The fruit is in the form of a pear.

Soil and situation: likes very well-drained, poor, porous soil – two parts sandy loam, one part crushed brick and one part silver sand – in a very sunny, dry position. Do not water until the soil becomes dry and dusty.

Design notes: just the plant for a themed Wild West garden with sand, dry sage, stone and lots of dry heat.

↕ 0.9–1.8 m (3–6 ft) ↔ 1.8–2.7 m (6–9 ft)

Perovskia 'Blue Spire'

Azure Sage UK/USA

Hardy, deciduous, shrubby plant with dense, greyish, downy leaves and violet-blue flowers in late summer.

Soil and situation: likes very well-drained, ordinary or poor soil in a sunny, dry position.

Design notes: although it can be trimmed into shape, it looks its best when allowed to mass and go semi-wild. Good choice for the edges of a dry garden when you want to create a silver-grey backdrop.

↕ 0.9–1.2 m (3–4 ft) ↔ 0.9–1.2 m (3–4 ft)

Yucca filamentosa

Adam's Needle UK/USA

Evergreen plant with short stems, long, strap-like leaves and small white or cream flowers on long stalks in mid- to late summer. There are many types, some subtropical and others desert.

Soil and situation: likes very well-drained, poor, porous, sandy soil in a very sunny, dry position.

Design notes: a good option for a dry garden or a Mediterranean garden.

↕ 0.9–1.8 m (3-6 ft) ↔ 0.9–1.5 m (3–5 ft)

OTHER ROCK, SCREE AND DESERT PLANTS

- *Aster turbinellus*: hardy perennial with small, spiky leaves and masses of violet, daisy-like flowers. Can cope with poor, dry, well-drained soil. Grows to a height of about 0.9–1.5 m (3–5 ft).

- *Cercis siliquastrum* (**Judas Tree**): hardy plant that can be grown as a single-stemmed tree or as a scraggy shrub. Has kidney-shaped, blue-green leaves and little, pink, ball-shaped flowers. Likes a poorish soil in a dry, sunny position – good for a Mediterranean garden. Can be kept as a low shrub or allowed to grow to 7.5 m (25 ft) or more.

- *Origanum laevigatum* '**Herrenhausen**' (**Oregano**): fully hardy plant with masses of purple-pink flowers and rosettes of evergreen, aromatic leaves. Likes a sunny, dry position.

- *Salvia sclarea* var. *turkestanica* (**Clary Sage**): short-lived perennial or biennial with a strong, slightly rank smell (see also page 61). Does well in a dry, sunny spot.

Water plants

There are plants for every wet and watery situation. From the outer reaches of the garden and working in towards the centre of the pond, you need: waterside plants to complement and shelter the pond, bog plants for the damp ground around the water's edge, emergent or marginal plants for the shallows, floating-leaf and deep-water plants for a whole range of depths, and aquatic plants that float and/or are completely or partially submerged.

How do I choose water plants?

WATER-GARDEN PLANTS AS DESIGN FEATURES

Water-garden plants are no more or less than plants that enjoy growing in, on or near water. They are a good choice if you want to have a natural wild pond, a meadow stream, a mountain brook or a Moorish pool, for example. In many ways, water plants control the pattern of planting, in as much as their needs are very specific. Although you can certainly choose what type of plants you want, you have very little choice when it comes to where they are going to fit in the watery scheme of things. Be aware that it is vital to buy plants to suit the diameter and depth of your pond. It is a good idea to start by getting one or two feature plants, and then, once they have taken hold, fill in between them with a few other, complementary, plants.

The joy of irises

If you love water gardens, you might become one of the growing number of enthusiasts who pack their gardens with irises, since irises and water go together perfectly.

A poet once said that irises 'come in three forms – beautiful, beautiful and more beautiful'.

Acorus calamus 'Variegatus'
Sweet Flag UK/USA

Hardy, herbaceous, aquatic plant with long, sword-like leaves and small, yellow flowers in summer.

Soil and situation: likes to have its roots in shallow water near the edge of a pool in a situation that is a mix of sun and shade.

Design notes: looks its best in a wild-type pond alongside such plants as irises, *Salix* (Willow) and rushes.

↕ 30–90 cm (1–3 ft) ↔ 60–90 cm (2–3 ft)

Astilbe chinensis 'Visions'
Goat's Beard UK/USA

Hardy herbaceous perennial with green leaves and masses of pink-purple flowers borne on tall, spiky stems in mid- to late summer. There are lots of other varieties to choose from in many different colours and heights.

Soil and situation: likes a deep, moist, loamy soil in a sunny or shaded position.

Design notes: a good option for a bog garden; perfect for the edge of a large natural pond running into a shady wood.

↕ 0.9–1.8 m (3–6 ft) ↔ 0.9–1.2 m (3–4 ft)

Cyperus
Umbrella Papyrus UK/USA

Umbrella Plant UK/USA

Tender perennial with long, spiky, grass-like leaves set on top of a tall stem – just like the ribs of an umbrella.

Soil and situation: likes a deep, rich, moist, loamy soil on the margins of water and a warm, sunny position.

Design notes: a good choice for growing in boggy ground alongside ponds and slow-moving streams, reminiscent of Egyptian scenes.

↕ 60–90 cm (2–3 ft) ↔ 60–90 cm (2–3 ft)

Eichhornia

Water Hyacinth UK/USA

Aquatic plant with round, glossy leaves. Can produce pale blue, hyacinth-like flowers in the right conditions.

Soil and situation: likes to be floating on the surface of the water with its long roots anchored in the mud at the bottom of the pond. Likes warmth and sun.

Design notes: while this is a good option for ponds, it is one of those plants that can swiftly grow out of control. That said, a carpet of Water Hyacinth floating on the warm waters of a pond looks very attractive.

↕ 15–23 cm (6–9 in) ↔ unlimited

Hosta crispula

Plantain Lily UK

Hosta USA

Hardy herbaceous perennial with variegated leaves and creamy white flowers on long stems.

Soil and situation: likes a deep, rich, moist, loamy soil in a warm, shady position.

Design notes: a good plant to have in the areas that run down to a bog garden – moist but not wet. Looks perfect set against a backdrop of trees; also a good choice for a Japanese-style water garden.

↕ 60–90 cm (2–3 ft) ↔ 60–90 cm (2–3 ft)

Nymphaea

Waterlily UK/USA

Hardy aquatic plants with floating leaves and beautiful multi-coloured flowers. There are hundreds of varieties to choose from and plants for every depth of water.

Soil and situation: likes a deep, rich, moist, loamy soil with at least 38 cm (15 in) of water above the roots, and must be in full sun. The ideal setting is a large pond at about 60 cm (2 ft) deep.

Design notes: this plant is essential for a water garden.

↕ 25–30 cm (10–12 in) ↔ 60–90 cm (2–3 ft)

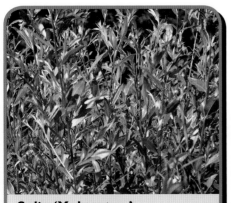

Salix 'Yelverton'

Willow UK/USA

Deciduous tree or shrub with slender, grey-green leaves and red-tinged stems. To create new plants, simply take pencil-length cuttings of ripened wood and push them into the ground.

Soil and situation: likes a moist, loamy soil next to water, in a warm, sunny position. Does not mind a flood situation, but dislikes waterlogged soil.

Design notes: if you want a natural pond, plant one or more around the fringes. This type is best cut back so that new stems grow up from the root base.

↕ 1.2–1.5 m (4–5 ft) ↔ 1.2–1.5 m (4–5 ft)

Zantedeschia

Arum Lily UK/USA

Calla UK/USA

Dramatic, herbaceous perennial with large, arrow-shaped leaves and large, wraparound, cream-white flowers.

Soil and situation: likes a deep, rich, moist to wet, loamy soil in a warm, sunny position.

Design notes: a good option for a bog garden – say where a pond overflows into an area of bog planting. It can even be used as a marginal with its roots set in the water. A dramatic plant – perfect for an exotic, lush effect.

↕ 60–90 cm (2–3 ft) ↔ 60–90 cm (2–3 ft)

OTHER WATER PLANTS

- *Azolla caroliniana* (**Fairy Moss**): free-floating, fast-growing perennial that has small rosettes of kidney-shaped leaves and produces small, white flowers; it will swiftly cover the surface of a pond.

- *Iris versicolor* (**Blue Flag Iris**): erect, deciduous perennial with green leaves and violet-blue flowers. Good for a boggy area.

- *Nuphar* (**Japanese Pond Lily**): beautiful perennial with floating, heart-shaped leaves and brilliant yellow flowers. Good for a deep-water pond with slow-moving water and plenty of sunshine. The leaves provide cover for fish as well as inhibiting the growth of algae by blocking out sunlight.

- *Ranunculus aquatilis* (**Water Buttercup**): pretty, delicate annual or perennial with small, green leaves and yellow-white flowers. Semi-submerged, it grows both on and under the water. A good choice for oxygenating the pond.

Bamboos and grasses

Apart from the fact that bamboos and grasses belong to the same family (bamboo is a fast-growing tropical or semi-tropical grass of the genus *Bambusa*), they are also grouped because they are used more for their foliage than their flowers, and because they simply look good together. If you want to create a garden that speaks of exotic places, a Japanese garden or a green-themed garden, bamboos and grasses are ideal candidates for the job.

BAMBOOS AND GRASSES AS DESIGN FEATURES

While bamboos and grasses are good for Asian-themed gardens, they are also a great option when you want to create a cool, quiet garden that features form and texture rather than colour. Bamboos and grasses invariably make good edge-of-patio plants in situations where the soil is likely to be well drained.

If you want to create a Japanese garden, or a modern 'meditation' or 'contemplation' garden, bamboos and grasses are the perfect plants to use. It has long been thought by Eastern artists, poets and mystics that the gentle movement and quiet rustling produced when eddies of air flow through bamboos and grasses is somehow uniquely calming and therapeutic, conducive to quiet reflection.

Grasses as design features

If you want to create a low-maintenance garden in a small space, the effect can be achieved by planting grasses in and around a terracotta pot and setting the whole against a backdrop of stones and gravel.

A beautiful arrangement of grasses and various ground-cover plants.

Deschampsia cespitosa 'Goldtau'

Tufted Hair Grass UK/USA

Tussock Grass UK/USA

Hardy, ornamental grass with tall, gold-bronze flowerheads emerging from tufted green foliage.

Soil and situation: likes a slightly moist soil in a sunny or shaded position.

Design notes: this grass makes a beautiful backdrop to water, and looks good in patio planters. A good choice for a Japanese garden. A large specimen is an impressive sight.

↕ 60–90 cm (2–3 ft) ↔ 60–90 cm (2–3 ft)

Miscanthus sinensis 'Morning Light'

Zebra Grass UK/USA

Hardy, ornamental grass with narrow, green, yellow- or silver-striped leaves.

Soil and situation: likes a deep, moist, loamy soil in a sunny or shaded position.

Design notes: a good option for areas that fringe a bog garden, and perfect for a bog garden that is overhung by young trees.

↕ 0.9–1.8 m (3–6 ft) ↔ 30–90 cm (1–3 ft)

Miscanthus sinensis 'Variegatus'

Hardy, ornamental grass with narrow, green, yellow- or silver-striped leaves.

Soil and situation: likes a deep, moist, loamy soil in a sunny or shaded position.

Design notes: a good option for bordering on a bog garden, perfect against a red brick wall, and ideal for a Japanese garden.

↕ 0.9–1.8 m (3–6 ft) ↔ 30–90 cm (1–3 ft)

Pennisetum

Bristle Grass UK/USA

Half-hardy, ornamental grass with narrow, silver-grey leaves.

Soil and situation: likes a well-drained soil in a sunny position.

Design notes: a good plant for a semi-dry garden – a patio, container, or a walled, Mediterranean-type garden. There are both compact and tall-growing types.

↕ 0.3–3 m (1–10 ft)　↔ 30–60 cm (1–2 ft)

Phyllostachys aureosulcata

Bamboo with wand-like, orange-yellow branches and pale green leaves. The stems are erect and densely crowded. There are several varieties.

Soil and situation: likes a deep, moist, loamy soil in a sunny or shaded, sheltered position; needs lots of water and hates cold winds.

Design notes: a good option when you want to have a medium-sized clump of bamboo. It is much favoured by designers of Japanese gardens.

↕ 3–4.5 m (10–15 ft)　↔ indefinite

Sasa veitchii
syn. *Arundinaria veitchii*

Kuma Bamboo Grass UK/USA

Hardy, low-growing bamboo with slender purple-green canes.

Soil and situation: likes a deep, moist soil in a sunny or shaded position.

Design notes: a good choice when you want a bamboo without too much height. The long leaves and the purple canes make a fine contrasting backdrop for grasses and dry-garden plants.

↕ 0.9–1.5 m (3–5 ft)　↔ indefinite

Stipa tenuissima

Feather Grass UK/USA

Hardy, ornamental grass with narrow, green leaves and feathery flowerheads.

Soil and situation: likes a well-drained soil in a sunny or shaded position.

Design notes: a good option for wild gardens, patio gardens, containers, as a backdrop to a small pond – anywhere where you want to achieve a delicate look. It looks its best when wafting in a gentle breeze.

↕ 60–90 cm (2–3 ft)　↔ 30–90 cm (1–3 ft)

Uncinia rubra

Red Grass UK/USA

Hardy, ornamental grass with narrow, green, red- or orange-striped leaves.

Soil and situation: likes a well-drained soil in a sunny or shaded position.

Design notes: a fine choice if you want a grass, yet at the same time you want to introduce a small amount of colour to offset the yellows and greens. This grass looks its best when set against a mulch of woodchip or leafmould.

↕ 30–60 cm (1–2 ft)　↔ 30–60 cm (1–2 ft)

OTHER BAMBOOS AND GRASSES

- **Coix lacryma-jobi (Christ's Tears/Job's Tears):** half-hardy grass with spear-shaped leaves. An excellent choice for a well-drained but moist spot in full sun.
- *Cortaderia selloana* (**Pampas Grass**): perennial, evergreen grass with slender leaves and tall, woody stems that bear fluffy, plume-like flowers. This plant makes a beautiful specimen for a very large pot or tub.
- *Hakonechloa macra* 'Alboaurea': hardy grass with a low, cascading habit, with narrow, variegated leaves. A good option for a low border around a patio, or a small detail within a Japanese garden.
- *Pleioblastus viridistriatus* (**Golden-haired Bamboo**): hardy, low-growing bamboo – a good choice for a container garden.
- *Phyllostachys nigra* (**Black-stemmed Bamboo**): hardy evergreen bamboo with green canes that turn to black within 2–3 years. Looks exotic – a good choice for a Japanese garden.

Container plants

**What are
my options?**

Maybe you want to enjoy gardening, but have only a balcony, a backyard, a patio, a barbecue area, a roof garden, a windowsill or a front doorstep to play with. The answer is to grow your plants in containers – these can be anything from mugs, buckets, bins and barrels to old teapots, tin baths and troughs – and put them in a place that catches the sun, at least for part of the day. Matching up the plant with the container is where the design comes in.

CONTAINER PLANTS AS DESIGN FEATURES

Just about any plant can be grown in a container – if the plant is compact enough and the container is big enough – and therefore the whole subject is as much about containers as it is about plants. From the designer's viewpoint, containers can be anything from a small vase through to a stone trough. Apart from the look of the actual container – its shape, colour, size and texture – using containers allows the designer to change space. One moment the garden is no more than a small courtyard garden, and the next there are containers everywhere – hanging on the walls, as window-boxes, hanging from chains and ropes, fixed to poles, stacked on shelves, grouped just inside the house. Suddenly the garden is much bigger and full of interest.

Portable patio planters

If you live in a rented house or flat (apartment) with a small courtyard where you want a garden and yet you want to take the plants with you when you move on, the answer is to grow everything in a range of pots and containers.

An attractive corner with most of the plants in containers, ready to go.

Armeria maritima
Sea Pink UK/USA

Thrift UK/USA
Hardy, evergreen plant of low, tufted growth, with brilliant, fluffy pink flowers.

Soil and situation: likes a light, well-drained, sandy soil in a sunny position. Does well in maritime districts.

Design notes: a good plant for seaside areas – on balconies and patios – especially in flat stone troughs and in rock-type containers. Ideal for an enclosed garden or a themed Mediterranean garden.

⬆ 30–60 cm (1–2 ft)　↔ creeping

Chamaerops humilis
Fan Palm UK/USA
Very attractive, dwarf-growing palm with slender leaves fanning out from spiny stalks, and small, yellow flowers in early spring.

Soil and situation: likes a fibrous loam with plenty of grit. Does really well in warm, sheltered, coastal areas, but must be generously watered.

Design notes: just right for a dry-type Mediterranean garden. Looks good alongside grasses and bamboos – very exciting with a white-rendered wall as a backdrop. It needs a huge pot.

⬆ 1.2–1.8 m (4–6 ft)　↔ 1.2–1.8 m (4–6 ft)

Erigeron
Fleabane UK/USA

Summer Starwort UK/USA
Hardy, herbaceous perennial that produces pale purple and/or deep lavender, daisy-like flowers.

Soil and situation: likes a light, well-drained, sandy soil in a sunny position.

Design notes: a very attractive, old-fashioned plant that looks just right in a low, flat container. Good choice for a seaside garden.

⬆ 30–60 cm (1–2 ft)　↔ 30–60 cm (1–2 ft)

Gazania
Treasure Flower UK/USA

Half-hardy perennial that belongs to the daisy family, with brilliant orange-yellow flowers in summer.

Soil and situation: likes well-drained soil in a sunny or shaded position.

Design notes: does well in a container, as long as it is positioned in full sun. The colour is striking – good for a small Mediterranean courtyard garden.

↕ 30 cm (1 ft) ↔ 30 cm (1 ft)

Salvia officinalis
Sage UK/USA

Very large group of hardy plants, some of which can be used as culinary herbs, with small, green leaves and brilliant blue flowers.

Soil and situation: likes a light, well-drained soil in a sunny position.

Design notes: a great option for container planting; perfect for a small kitchen porch garden.

↕ 30–90 cm (1–3 ft) ↔ 30 cm (1 ft)

Sedum
Stonecrop UK/USA

Very large group of hardy succulents. A full, plump cushion of small, yellow flowers is produced in summer, and brilliantly coloured leaves in autumn.

Soil and situation: likes a light, well-drained soil in a sunny position.

Design notes: a particularly good option for container planting, in that it fills the container to overflowing, to the extent that the plant and the container become an integrated form. Just about every part of the plant will grow where it falls – leaves, roots and seeds.

↕ 7.5–45 cm (3–18 in) ↔ 30–90 cm (1–3 ft)

Stipa arundinacea
Feather Grass UK/USA

Hardy, ornamental grass with a beautiful gold-purple tinge to the feathery heads.

Soil and situation: likes a well-drained soil in a sunny or shaded position.

Design notes: although this particular grass is more vigorous than most, it is still a good option for a container. It looks its best alongside other grasses on a patio.

↕ 60–90 cm (2–3 ft) ↔ 30–90 cm (1–3 ft)

Thymus
Common Creeping Thyme UK/USA
Thyme UK/USA

Group of hardy sub-shrubs and herbaceous plants, some of which can be used as culinary herbs, with small, green leaves and brilliant blue, heather-like flowers. There are lots of types – Lemon Thyme, Orange-scented Thyme, Seed Cake Thyme and more.

Soil and situation: likes a light, well-drained soil in a sunny position.

Design notes: a good option for a container just outside the back door – perfect if you enjoy cooking.

↕ 30–45 cm (12–18 in) ↔ creeping

OTHER CONTAINER PLANTS

- **Bulbs:** winter-, spring- and summer-flowering bulbs all do well and look great in containers.
- **Climbers:** Clematis, *Lathyrus odoratus* (Sweet Pea) and plants like *Humulus lupulus* (Hop) all also do well in containers, but need supports.
- *Cortaderia selloana* (**Pampas Grass**): perennial evergreen grass with slender leaves and tall woody stems. It needs a large pot, and is good for a large patio.
- *Phyllostachys nigra* (**Black-stemmed Bamboo**): hardy evergreen with green canes that turn to black within 2–3 years. Looks exotic.
- **Small trees:** these can do well in good-sized containers. You could either choose dwarf conifers and *Acers* (Maples), or choose full-sized trees and treat them in much the same way as bonsai by top- and root-pruning to keep them small.
- **Vegetables:** potatoes, tomatoes and salad crops are good options, just right for a small-yard kitchen garden.

Herbs

Herbs are plants that have traditionally been grown for medicinal, cosmetic and culinary uses. This book focuses on well-known, safe-to-use culinary herbs such as Sage, Rosemary and Borage, and herbs like Lavender that smell good. Other herbs are illustrated, but only for their ornamental qualities. Be warned: if you wish to turn any plant that is unknown to you into a tea, rub, balm, poultice or anything else, you must research it thoroughly first.

HERBS AS DESIGN FEATURES

If, just for a moment, we forget about the culinary aspect of herbs and simply focus on what they look and smell like, then you can see that there are a lot of design options. You could grow them in containers so that they are close to hand, in a traditional knot-type garden with various colours and forms making patterns, in a small confined space so that you can enjoy their aromatic qualities, in groups – all thymes, all mints, or whatever you like – and so on. There are lots of options. All that said, however, the traditional approach of growing herbs in a small, dedicated area – so you can pop out from the kitchen and pick fresh herbs for the cooking pot – does take a bit of beating. There are lots of suppliers who specialize in herbs, selling both plants and related items, so check for those in your local area.

Fresh herbs for the taking

Herbs in pots and containers placed close to the kitchen door are a great idea. They look good, they smell good, and they are handy when you come to do the cooking.

Fresh herbs ready for picking are hard to beat.

Borago officinalis

Borage UK/USA

Hardy, fragrant annual with green-grey leaves and bright blue flowers, grown both for its leaves and its looks.

Soil and situation: likes well-drained soil in a sunny, sheltered position.

Design notes: while Borage looks fine set alongside other herbs like Lavender and Rosemary, it looks particularly good when it is planted in a wild garden and allowed to do its own thing.

 ↕ 30–60 cm (1–2 ft) ↔ 30–60 cm (1–2 ft)

Carlina acaulis

Carlina Thistle UK/USA

Hardy plant with a thistle-like appearance and a large, spiky, ball-shaped, purple flowerhead. It was an important herb in the past, but is no longer used as one.

Soil and situation: likes a light, well-drained soil in a sunny position.

Design notes: an excellent option for a walled garden. The height of the plant and the dramatic appearance of the flowerheads makes it a good backdrop plant. It would look fine in a colour-themed bed.

↕ 30–60 cm (1–2 ft) ↔ 30 cm (1 ft)

Foeniculum vulgare

Fennel UK/USA

Hardy perennial with feathery, green leaves on long, bamboo-like stems.

Soil and situation: likes well-drained soil in a sunny, sheltered position, but seems to grow just about anywhere.

Design notes: not only is Fennel a very easy-to-grow herb, but it is a beautifully tall and exotic plant, more like a grass or bamboo than anything else. Looks good in a walled garden, as a backdrop to the herb bed. Also a good container plant.

↕ 0.9–1.8 m (3–6 ft) ↔ 60–90 cm (2–3 ft)

Lavandula 'Hidcote'

Lavender UK/USA

Hardy, evergreen shrub with small, silver-grey leaves and blue flowers in summer. The particular blue is so singular that it has come to be called 'lavender blue'.

Soil and situation: likes a well-drained, sandy loam-type soil in a sunny, sheltered position.

Design notes: there are many other varieties of Lavender to choose from.

↕ 30–60 cm (1–2 ft) ↔ 30–60 cm (1–2 ft)

Myrrhis odorata

Sweet Cicely UK/USA

Hardy, fragrant perennial herb with fern-like leaves, small, white, multiple flowers, and long, dark brown fruits.

Soil and situation: likes any well-drained soil in a sunny, sheltered position.

Design notes: this plant is fragrant in all its parts. The leaves are aromatic, the fruits have a sweet smell, and the whole plant has a fragrance or odour that has been likened to that of myrrh. This is a good option for an enclosed courtyard garden or a container garden. It looks good alongside Fennel.

↕ 0.9–1.2 m (3–4 ft) ↔ 30–60 cm (1–2 ft)

Rosmarinus officinalis

Rosemary UK/USA

Hardy, shrubby, fragrant plant, with narrow leaves – glossy green on top and greeny white on the underside – with small, blue flowers.

Soil and situation: likes a light, well-drained, sandy loam-type soil in a sunny, sheltered position. Thrives in coastal areas.

Design notes: Rosemary can be kept tight and compact or 'let go' to make a scraggy shrub. It looks particularly attractive in the form of a low hedge, perhaps round the herb garden.

↕ 0.6–2.1 m (2–7 ft) ↔ 0.9–1.2 m (3–4 ft)

Ruta graveolens

Rue UK/USA

Herb of Grace UK/USA

Shrub-like and hardy, with deeply divided, blue-green leaves, and terminal clusters of yellow flowers in summer.

Soil and situation: likes a light, well-drained soil in a sunny position.

Design notes: this plant would look good anywhere, but especially in a colour-themed bed.

↕ 30–90 cm (1–3 ft) ↔ 30 cm (1 ft)

Salvia sclarea

Clary Sage UK/USA

Hardy biennial with large, hairy leaves, and blue and white, tubular flowers borne in late summer.

Soil and situation: likes a light, well-drained soil in a sunny position.

Design notes: would look good anywhere – in a container, in a walled garden, growing wild in a meadow, let go as a scraggy shrub, or in a colour-themed bed.

↕ 30–90 cm (1–3 ft) ↔ 30 cm (1 ft)

OTHER HERBS

- *Anethum graveolens* (Dill): aromatic annual with hollow stems, delicate, finely divided foliage, and umbels of tiny yellow flowers in summer. Grows to a height of 60 cm (2 ft).
- *Artemisia dracunculus* (Tarragon): shrubby plant grown for its leaves – good in a salad or in a dressing. Has woody stems, narrow leaves and inconspicuous flowers. Grows to a height of about 90 cm (3 ft).
- *Mentha* spp. (Mint): small group of fragrant, hardy perennials often used in cooking. The various types, such as Common Mint, Spearmint, Apple Mint and Pineapple Mint, each give off a characteristic fragrance when the leaves are bruised. A good swift-growing option for a container garden, but can be invasive in borders unless roots are contained.
- *Satureja* (Winter Savory): hardy, aromatic-leaved herb with small, pale green leaves and small, lilac-coloured flowers. Used to flavour soups and stews. Good for a herb garden or as a specimen plant in a container.

Fruit and vegetables

Can edible crops look attractive?

Should you wish to grow fruit and vegetables, there are many different ways in which you can do it. You could have a screened-off area with long rows for easy access, lots of small, raised beds that you can walk around and stretch over, single plants in among the flower beds, a mixture of vegetables, herbs and salad crops grown in a pattern of small, geometrical beds, plants in containers on your patio, or a whole walled garden, to mention just a few of the possibilities.

FRUIT AND VEGETABLES AS DESIGN FEATURES

Most people somehow forget that fruit and vegetables are visually exciting and attractive in much the same way as a rose. What could be more beautiful than a tomato plant loaded with fruit, or an orchard tree bowed down with Victoria plums, or a good fat marrow? Of course, we know that all these items taste very good, but the trick for the garden designer is not exactly to forget about the eating bit but to focus in on the whole package – the decorative potential plus the food potential. If you look at the items on this spread – tomatoes, aubergines (eggplants), beans, lettuces, courgettes (zucchini), apples and figs – you can instantly see that they would make a wonderful contribution to any garden, a joy to the eye as well as the stomach!

Fresh fruit and vegetables among the flowers

Strawberries are often grown in planters, but why not go one step further and grow things like chard, lettuces and radishes in among the flowers?

Tomato
Tender plant with broad, green leaves and bright red fruits.

Soil and situation: likes deep, rich, well-dug soil, with lots of well-rotted organic matter worked into it, in a sunny, sheltered position.

Design notes: there are lots of tomato types to choose from and lots of ways to grow them – as bushes, up strings or wires, in containers, or as low, dwarf bushes that bow down so that the fruit is cupped in a nest of straw – a bit like strawberries. Could look really attractive as a backdrop to, say, a herb bed.

Aubergine/Eggplant
Tender plant with broad, green leaves and large, purple or white fruits.

Soil and situation: likes much the same conditions as the tomato – deep, rich, well-dug soil, with lots of well-rotted organic matter, in a sunny, sheltered position.

Design notes: just as with tomatoes, you can grow them as bushes, up strings or wires, in containers, or as low, dwarf bushes that bow down so that the fruit is cupped in a nest of straw. They do well against the foot of a sunny wall, or you could create a cottage kitchen-garden effect and grow them among the flower beds.

Beans
Semi-hardy perennial, usually treated as an annual, with broad, green leaves, pea-like flowers, and clusters of long pods. There are lots of types to choose from – broad (fava) beans, French beans and runner beans.

Soil and situation: likes deep, rich, well-dug soil, with lots of well-rotted organic matter worked into it, in a sunny, sheltered position.

Design notes: most beans produce masses of decorative foliage, which can be useful for covering an ugly wall or structure.

Lettuce

Range of semi-hardy and hardy plants eaten in salads.

Soil and situation: generally likes deep, rich, well-dug soil, with lots of well-rotted organic matter, in a sunny, sheltered position.

Design notes: apart from types like round cabbage lettuce and pointed Cos, that are just cut off and taken to the kitchen, there are many other types, such as Lamb's lettuce, American cress and rocket, that are treated as nip-and-eat plants, where leaves are taken as and when required, so there is no reason why lettuces cannot be grown among flowers. Some even make good ground cover.

Courgette/Zucchini

Tender plant with broad, green leaves, dramatic, trumpet-shaped, yellow flowers, and marrow-like fruits.

Soil and situation: likes deep, rich, well-dug soil, with lots of well-rotted organic matter, in a sunny, sheltered position. Best grown on a mound of soil.

Design notes: there are lots of marrow-type vegetables to choose from. Courgettes make very dramatic, trailing plants. If you put them in a sheltered spot, the plants will send off tumbling runners and masses of luxuriant leafage with lots of flowers and fruits. They are good near a patio, and even better within reach of a barbecue.

Apple

Hardy tree with green leaves and characteristically firm, green and red-yellow fruits.

Soil and situation: likes deep, rich, well-drained soil in a sunny, sheltered position. Does not like waterlogged soil.

Design notes: the trees can be free-standing, grown against walls, trained over pergolas and frames, grown as small bushes, and so on. In the modern small garden, they are best grown hard up against a wall.

Fig

Tree with hand-shaped leaves and pear-shaped fruits.

Soil and situation: likes ordinary, well-drained soil, with the addition of crushed mortar rubble at a depth of about 90 cm (3 ft), in a sunny, sheltered position. Make sure the roots are constricted, to contain their spread.

Design notes: a great tree for a sheltered, walled garden. If you are more interested in foliage than fruit, miss out on the rubble and enrich the soil.

OTHER FRUITS AND VEGETABLES

- **Cucumber:** can be grown in much the same way as tomatoes – either as bushes or trained up wires. Any sheltered, sunny wall or fence will do. They have lots of attractive foliage as well as yellow flowers. Good for a children's area – the kids can pick and eat the cucumbers when they are small and tender.
- **Pea:** another good plant to have growing near the barbecue area. If you get everything right, you may end up being able to cook your meat or fish, and then serve it up with fresh peas, lettuce leaves, lightly grilled (broiled) courgettes (zucchini), and perhaps a few radishes, all right there to hand.
- **Plum:** a good companion for an apple tree. A Victoria plum tree heavily bowed down with fruit is a beautiful sight – just the thing to have on one side of a sitting area.
- **Potato:** a great plant that is relatively easy to grow, and that has lots of foliage, pretty flowers, and of course all the delicious potatoes just hiding under the ground and waiting to be harvested and eaten. Potatoes are another perfect subject for a children's garden – if you want your kids to eat these vegetables, then let them have the fun of growing a few plants themselves.
- **Radish:** radishes are another good option for a children's garden. They can be sown and cropped in three weeks – this is perfect for children who always want to see swift results.
- **Spinach Beet/Perpetual Spinach:** hardy plant with green leaves tinged with red, yellow or orange. Looks good and grows vigorously. This is ideal for a children's garden; they may not like stewed cabbage-like leaves, but they will like their very own spinach leaves, lightly steamed, dribbled with tomato sauce and served with fresh bread and butter.
- **Strawberries:** low-growing plants with nettle-like leaves and plump red fruits. Strawberries do well as ground cover. Can be grown in planters, windowboxes and hanging-baskets.

Glossary

Aggregate Loose mixture of pebbles crushed stone and sand in concrete; similar to ballast.

Aligning Setting one component part against another in order to obtain the best fit.

Annuals Plants that live out their life (flower, set seed and die) in a single growing season.

Backfilling Filling a cavity, behind a wall or in a foundation trench hole, in order to bring the earth level up.

Bedding Pressing a stone, slab or brick into a bed or layer of wet mortar and ensuring that it is level.

Biennials Plants that flower and die in the second growing season.

Bog garden Part of the garden, usually close to a pond, where the soil is permanently wet or damp.

Bog plants Plants that will grow with their roots in wet or damp soil. Because some plants will grow in anything from moist ground to shallow water, there is sometimes confusion between bog plants that enjoy very wet ground and emergent plants that enjoy growing in the outer margins of a pond.

Buttering Using a trowel to cover a piece of stone or brick with wet mortar just prior to setting it in position.

Butting Pushing one component hard up against another in order to obtain a good flush fit with both faces touching.

Centring Setting a measurement or component part on the centre of another, or measuring a length or width to find the centre.

Cladding Covering a frame with a layer of wood.

Compacting Using a hammer and/ or the weight of your body to press down on a layer of sand, earth or hardcore.

Course Term used to describe the horizontal layers of brick or stone within a wall.

Coursing General term describing the process of bedding stone and brick in mortar in order to build a course.

Curing time Time taken for mortar or concrete to become firm and stable. 'Part cured' means that the mortar or concrete is firm enough to take a small amount of weight.

Damping Wetting bricks, slabs or stone just prior to bedding them in or on mortar.

Deciduous Describes plants that shed their leaves at the end of the growing season.

Dressing Using a hammer, chisel, or trowel to trim a stone to a level, smooth, or textured finish.

Evergreen Describes plants that retain their leaves for more than one growing season.

Exotic plants Plants that are not native to temperate climates, and have a striking or unusual appearance.

Finishing Term describing the whole procedure at the end of a project of pointing, washing down, planting and so on, in order to complete the job.

Floating Using a metal, plastic or wooden float to skim wet concrete or mortar to a smooth and level finish.

Hardy Describes a plant that is able to withstand year-round conditions, heavy frost, heavy rainfall and dry summers.

Inspiration All the background interests and passions that give shape and form to a design.

Levelling Using a spirit-level to decide whether or not a structure or component part is horizontally parallel to the ground, or vertically at right angles to the ground, and then going on to make adjustments to bring the component into line.

Marking out Using items such as a pencil, rule, square, compass, pegs and string to mark out an area on the ground, in readiness for digging out, or otherwise taking the project forward.

Mulch Covering of bark chippings, pebbles, sheet plastic, manure or other material applied in a layer over the soil in order to conserve moisture and cut back on weed growth.

Orientation How the house and plot are positioned in relation to the sun.

Perennials Plants, usually woody or herbaceous, that live for three or more seasons.

Permanent features Anything that cannot or should not be moved – the house, boundaries, mature trees, rocky outcrops and so on.

Planning The whole procedure of considering the project, looking at the materials, making drawings, working out amounts and costs, prior to actually starting the project.

Pointing Using a trowel, stick, or a tool of your choice to bring the mortar joints to the desired finish.

Raking out Using a trowel to rake out mortar from between courses, so that the edges or brick or stone are seen to best advantage.

Sighting Judging by eye, in order to determine whether or not a structure is level or true.

Soakaway A hole or pit filled with loose rubble or hardcore into which water drains.

Sourcing Process of asking questions, by various means of communication, or doing research in order to make decisions as to the best source for materials.

Squaring Technique of marking out with a set-square and or spirit-level so that one surface or structure is at right angles to another.

Striking Using a length of wood to compact and level wet concrete.

Tamping To pack down tightly with successive blows or taps.

Trial run Running through a procedure of setting out some part of a structure in order to discover whether or not the envisaged project or technique is feasible.

Trimming Bringing wood, brick or stone to a good finish.

Wire brushing Using a wire bristled brush to remove dry mortar from the face of the brick, slab or stone – as with a wall, or the surface of a path or patio.

Workboards Wooden boards – sheets of plywood – that can be put down at the start of a project to protect the ground.

Index

Acknowledgments

AG&G Books would like to thank **Richo Cech** of **Horizon Herbs, LLC** for supplying photographs of their herbs. Horizon Herbs is a family-run farm in Southern Oregon, USA that grows over 700 medicinal plant species. They focus on seed work and sell nursery stock. Contact Horizon Herbs, PO Box 69, 3350 Cedar Flat Road, Williams, OR 97544, telephone (541) 8466704, www.horizonherbs. com for a free catalogue. Richo Cech is the author of *Making Plant Medicine* (2000) and *Growing At-Risk Medicinal Herbs* (2002). AG&G Books would like to thank **Thompson & Morgan**, Quality Seedsmen Since 1855, *brings the finest quality flower and vegetable seed and flower plant varieties to the home gardener*, Thompson & Morgan (UK) Ltd, Poplar Lane, Ipswich, Suffolk, IP8 3BU. AG&G Books would like to thank Stephen Evans of **Golden Days Garden Centre**, Back Lane, Appley Bridge, Standish, Wigan, WN6 8RS, Tel. 01257 423355, goldendaysgardencentre@btconnect.com and Manchester Road, Cheadle, Cheshire, SK8 2NZ, Tel. 0161 4283098, goldendays@ btconnect.com, www.goldendaysgardencentre.com. AG&G Books would also like to thank the RHS Gardens at **Hyde Hall**, Rettendon, Chelmsford, Essex, England and at **Wisley**, Woking, Surrey, England. Photographs: AG&G Books (pages 1, 3, 6, 8, 20, 22, 24, 25, 28, 32, 34, 36, 40, 42, 44, 45, 46, 47, 48, 53, 54, 55, 56, 57, 58, 59, 60, 61, 63, 65TL and BL, 66, 67, 68, 69 TC, BL and BC, 70BC and BR, 71, 72, 73, 74BL and BR, 75TL and TR and 77), David Squire (pages 62BM, 64BR, 69TR, 70BL and 76BL and BR), Golden Days Garden Centre (page 69 TL and TR), Horizon Herbs (pages 74BC, 75TC, BL AND BC), and Thompson & Morgan (pages 62BR, 64BL and BC, 65TC and TR and 76BC).